W9-BJP-459

GOD'S PROMISES
for your every need

NASHVILLE

A Thomas Nelson Company

GOD'S PROMISES FOR YOUR EVERY NEED
Copyright © 1988, 1995 by World Publishing, Inc.
All rights reserved.

Copyright © 1999 by J. Countryman,
a division of Thomas Nelson, Inc.,
Nashville, TN 37214

Scripture quotations are from
The Holy Bible, King James Version.

Library of Congress Cataloging-in-Publication Data.

God's promises for your every need.
p.   cm.
ISBN 0-8499-51321 (bonded leather)
ISBN 0-8499-51305 (trade paper)
1. God—Promises—Biblical teaching. 2. Bible—Use.
I. Word Publishing
BS680.P68G63 1995
248.4—dc20

95-11754
CIP

Printed in Belgium

Preface

The Word of God establishes the family as the most important Christian social unit in our society and gives us guidance for proper relationships so that we might be everything God chooses for us , both individually and corporately. This wonderful scriptural guide will help you learn more about the promises for your family, God's guidance for a better family relationship, and how God truly wants to bless and direct every Christian family for His Glory.

Contents

7.   Truth From The Bible About • 251

8.   What You Can Do To • 311

9.   God's Plan of Salvation • 331

Jesus Is Your. . .

Saviour

Not by works of righteousness which we have done, but according to his mercy he saved us, by the washing of regeneration, and renewing of the Holy Ghost;

Which he shed on us abundantly through Jesus Christ our Saviour;

Titus 3:5,6

And we have seen and do testify that the Father sent the Son to be the Saviour of the world.

I John 4:14

And my spirit hath rejoiced in God my Saviour.

Luke 1:47

...for we have heard him ourselves, and know that this is indeed the Christ, the Saviour of the world.

John 4:42b

For the Son of man is come to seek and to save that which was lost.

Luke 19:10

For God so loved the world, that he gave his only begotten Son, that whosoever believeth in him should not perish, but have everlasting life.

John 3:16

Being justified freely by his grace through the redemption that is in Christ Jesus:

Whom God hath set forth to be a propitiation through faith in his blood, to declare his righteousness for the remission of sins that are past, through the forbearance of God;

Romans 3:24,25

But God, who is rich in mercy, for his great love wherewith he loved us,

Even when we were dead in sins, hath quickened us together with Christ, (by grace ye are saved;)

Ephesians 2:4,5

Verily, verily, I say unto you, He that believeth on me hath everlasting life.

John 6:47

For by grace are ye saved through faith; and that not of yourselves: it is the gift of God:

Not of works, lest any man should boast.

Ephesians 2:8,9

That if thou shalt confess with thy mouth the Lord Jesus, and shalt believe in thine heart that God hath raised him from the dead, thou shalt be saved.

Romans 10:9

Therefore if any man be in Christ, he is a new creature: old things are passed away; behold, all things are become new.

II Corinthians 5:17

Who hath saved us, and called us with an holy calling, not according to our works, but according to his own purpose and grace, which was given us in Christ Jesus before the world began,

II Timothy 1:9

Nevertheless he saved them for his name's sake, that he might make his mighty power to be known.

Psalm 106:8

Lord

Wherefore God also hath highly exalted him, and given him a name which is above every name:

That at the name of Jesus every knee should bow, of things in heaven, and things in earth, and things under the earth;

And that every tongue should confess that Jesus Christ is Lord, to the glory of God the Father.

Philippians 2:9-11

That if thou shalt confess with thy mouth the Lord Jesus, and shalt believe in thine heart that God hath raised him from the dead, thou shalt be saved.

For with the heart man believeth unto righteousness; and with the mouth confession is made unto salvation.

Romans 10:9, 10

And why call ye me, Lord, Lord, and do not the things which I say?

Luke 6:46

Neither yield ye your members as instruments of unrighteousness unto sin: but yield yourselves unto God, as those that are alive from the dead, and your members as instruments of righteousness unto God.

For sin shall not have dominion over you: for ye are not under the law, but under grace.

What then? shall we sin, because we are not under the law, but under grace? God forbid.

Know ye not, that to whom ye yield yourselves servants to obey, his servants ye are to whom ye obey; whether of sin unto death, or of obedience unto righteousness?

Romans 6:14-16

I beseech you therefore, brethren, by the mercies of God, that ye present your bodies a living sacrifice, holy, acceptable unto God, which is your reasonable service.

And be not conformed to this world: but be ye transformed by the renewing of your mind, that ye may prove what is that good, and acceptable, and perfect, will of God.

Romans 12:1, 2

What? know ye not that your body is the temple of the Holy Ghost which is in you, which you have of God, and ye are not your own?

For ye are bought with a price: therefore glorify God in your body, and in your spirit, which are God's.

I Corinthians 6:19, 20

Therefore let all the house of Israel know assuredly, that God hath made that same Jesus, whom ye have crucified, both Lord and Christ.

Acts 2:36

For whether we live, we live unto the Lord; and whether we die, we die unto the Lord: whether we live therefore, or die, we are the Lord's.

Romans 14:8

Blessed be the Lord, who daily loadeth us with benefits, even the God of our salvation. Selah.

Psalm 68:19

But it is good for me to draw near to God: I have put my trust in the Lord God, that I may declare all thy works.

Psalm 73:28

For thou, Lord, art good, and ready to forgive; and plenteous in mercy unto all them that call upon thee.

Psalm 86:5

For the Lord God will help me; therefore shall I not be confounded: therefore have I set my face like a flint, and I know that I shall not be ashamed.

Isaiah 50:7

And thou shalt love the Lord thy God with all thy heart, and with all thy soul, and with all thy mind, and with all thy strength: this is the first commandment.

Mark 12:30

For David speaketh concerning him, I foresaw the Lord always before my face, for he is on my right hand, that I should not be moved.

Acts 2:25

JESUS IS YOUR
Love

But God commendeth his love toward us, in that, while we were yet sinners, Christ died for us.

Romans 5:8

For God so loved the world that he gave his only begotten Son, that whosoever believeth in him should not perish, but have everlasting life.

John 3:16

Beloved, let us love one another: for love is of God; and every one that loveth is born of God, and knoweth God.

He that loveth not knoweth not God; for God is love.

In this was manifested the love of God toward us, because that God sent his only begotten Son into the world, that we might live through him.

Herein is love, not that we loved God, but that he loved us, and sent his Son to be the propitiation for our sins.

Beloved, if God so loved us, we ought also to love one another.

No man hath seen God at any time. If we love one another, God dwelleth in us, and his love is perfected in us.

I John 4:7-12

And we have known and believed the love that God hath to us.

God is love; and he that dwelleth in love dwelleth in God, and God in him.

We love him, because he first loved us.
I John 4:16, 19

As the Father hath loved me, so have I loved you: continue ye in my love.

If ye keep my commandments, ye shall abide in my love; even as I have kept my Father's commandments, and abide in his love.

These things have I spoken unto you, that my joy might remain in you, and that your joy might be full.

This is my commandment, That ye love one another, as I have loved you.

Greater love hath no man than this, that a man lay down his life for his friends.

These things I command you, that ye love one another.
John 15:9-13, 17

That Christ may dwell in your hearts by faith; that ye, being rooted and grounded in love,

May be able to comprehend with all saints what is the breadth, and length, and depth, and height;

And to know the love of Christ, which passeth knowledge, that ye might be filled with all the fulness of God.

Ephesians 3:17-19

I love them that love me; and those that seek me early shall find me.

Proverbs 8:17

The Lord hath appeared of old unto me, saying, Yea, I have loved thee with an everlasting love: therefore with loving-kindness have I drawn thee.

Jeremiah 31:3

And I will betroth thee unto me for ever; yea, I will betroth thee unto me in righteousness, and in judgment, and in loving-kindness, and in mercies.

Hosea 2:19

He that hath my commandments, and keepeth them, he it is that loveth me: and he that loveth me shall be loved of my Father, and I will love him, and will manifest myself to him.

John 14:21

Yet the Lord will command his loving-kindness in the day-time, and in the night his song shall be with me, and my prayer unto the God of my life.

Psalm 42:8

And now abideth faith, hope, charity, these three; but the greatest of these is charity.

I Corinthians 13:13

For I am persuaded, that neither death, nor life, nor angels, nor principalities, nor powers, nor things present, nor things to come,

Nor height, nor depth, nor any other creature, shall be able to separate us from the love of God, which is in Christ Jesus our Lord.

Romans 8:38, 39

JESUS IS YOUR
Peace

Thou wilt keep him in perfect peace, whose mind is stayed on thee: because he trusteth in thee.

Isaiah 26:3

But now in Christ Jesus ye who sometimes were far off are made nigh by the Blood of Christ.

For he is our peace, who hath made both one, and hath broken down the middle wall of partition between us;

Ephesians 2:13, 14

For unto us a child is born, unto us a son is given: and the government shall be upon his shoulder: and his name shall be called Wonderful, Counsellor, The mighty God, The everlasting Father, The Prince of Peace.

Of the increase of his government and peace there shall be no end, upon the throne of David, and upon his kingdom, to order it, and to establish it with judgment and with justice from henceforth even for ever. The zeal of the Lord of hosts will perform this.

Isaiah 9:6, 7

And the God of peace shall bruise Satan under your feet shortly. The grace of our Lord Jesus Christ be with you. Amen.

Romans 16:20

Lord, thou wilt ordain peace for us: for thou also hast wrought all our works in us.

Isaiah 26:12

Those things, which ye have both learned, and received, and heard, and seen in me, do: and the God of peace shall be with you.

Philippians 4:9

Therefore being justified by faith, we have peace with God through our Lord Jesus Christ:

Romans 5:1

And let the peace of God rule in your hearts, to the which also ye are called in one body; and be ye thankful.

Colossians 3:15

I will both lay me down in peace, and sleep: for thou, Lord, only makest me dwell in safety.

Psalm 4:8

The Lord will give strength unto his people; the Lord will bless his people with peace.

Psalm 29:11

Peace, I leave with you, my peace I give unto you: not as the world giveth, give I unto you. Let not your heart be troubled, neither let it be afraid.

John 14:27

Be careful for nothing; but in every thing by prayer and supplication with thanksgiving let your requests be made known unto God.

And the peace of God, which passeth all understanding, shall keep your hearts and minds through Christ Jesus.

Philippians 4:6, 7

JESUS IS YOUR
Forgiveness

To the praise of the glory of his grace, wherein he hath made us accepted in the beloved.

In whom we have redemption through his blood, the forgiveness of sins, according to the riches of his grace;

Ephesians 1:6, 7

Thou hast forgiven the iniquity of thy people, thou hast covered all their sin. Selah.

Psalm 85:2

Therefore if any man be in Christ, he is a new creature: old things are passed away; behold, all things are become new.

II Corinthians 5:17

As far as the east is from the west, so far hath he removed our transgressions from us.

Psalm 103:12

My little children, these things write I unto you, that ye sin not. And if any man sin, we have an advocate with the Father, Jesus Christ the righteous:

I John 2:1

If we confess our sins, he is faithful and just to forgive us our sins, and to cleanse us from all unrighteousness.

I John 1:9

For I will be merciful to their unrighteousness, and their sins and their iniquities will I remember no more.

Hebrews 8:12

Let the wicked forsake his way, and the unrighteous man his thoughts: and let him return unto the Lord, and he will have mercy upon him; and to our God, for he will abundantly pardon.

Isaiah 55:7

Forbearing one another, and forgiving one another, if any man have a quarrel against any: even as Christ forgave you, so also do ye.

Colossians 3:13

And when ye stand praying, forgive, if ye have ought against any: that your Father also which is in heaven may forgive you your trespasses.

Mark 11:25

And you, being dead in your sins and the uncircumcision of your flesh, hath he quickened together with him, having forgiven you all trespasses;

Colossians 2:13

And I will cleanse them from all their iniquity, whereby they have sinned against me; and I will pardon all their iniquities whereby they have sinned, and whereby they have transgressed against me.

Jeremiah 33:8

Come now, and let us reason together, saith the Lord: Though your sins be as scarlet, they shall be as white as snow; though they be red like crimson, they shall be as wool.

Isaiah 1:18

I, even I, am he that blotteth out thy transgressions for mine own sake, and will not remember thy sins.

Isaiah 43:25

Blessed is he whose transgression is forgiven, whose sin is covered.
Blessed is the man unto whom the Lord imputeth not iniquity, and in whose spirit there is no guile.

Psalm 32:1, 2

JESUS IS YOUR
Righteousness

For he hath made him to be sin for us, who knew no sin; that we might be made the righteousness of God in him.

II Corinthians 5:21

But of him are ye in Christ Jesus, who of God is made unto us wisdom, and righteousness, and sanctification, and redemption:

I Corinthians 1:30

And be found in him, not having mine own righteousness, which is of the law, but that which is through the faith of Christ, the righteousness which is of God by faith:

Philippians 3:9

Even as Abraham believed God, and it was accounted to him for righteousness.
Know ye therefore that they which are of faith, the same are the children of Abraham.

Galatians 3:6, 7

Even the righteousness of God which is by faith of Jesus Christ unto all and upon all them that believe: for there is no difference:

Romans 3:22

Being justified freely by his grace through the redemption that is in Christ Jesus:

Whom God hath set forth to be a propitiation through faith in his blood, to declare his righteousness for the remission of sins that are past, through the forbearance of God;

To declare, I say, at this time his righteousness: that he might be just, and the justifier of him which believeth in Jesus.

Romans 3:24-26

But to him that worketh not, but believeth on him that justifieth the ungodly, his faith is counted for righteousness.

Romans 4:5

For if by one man's offence death reigned by one; much more they which receive abundance of grace and of the gift of righteousness shall reign in life by one, Jesus Christ.

Romans 5:17

Not by works of righteousness which we have done, but according to his mercy he saved us, by the washing of regeneration, and renewing of the Holy Ghost;

Titus 3:5

For what the law could not do, in that it was weak through the flesh, God sending his own Son in the likeness of sinful flesh, and for sin, condemned sin in the flesh:

That the righteousness of the law might be fulfilled in us, who walk not after the flesh, but after the Spirit.

Romans 8:3, 4

What shall we say then? That the Gentiles, which followed not after righteousness, have attained to righteousness, even the righteousness which is of faith.

Romans 9:30

And if Christ be in you, the body is dead because of sin; but the Spirit is life because of righteousness.

Romans 8:10

For whom he did foreknow, he also did predestinate to be conformed to the image of his Son, that he might be the firstborn among many brethren.

Moreover whom he did predestinate, them he also called: and whom he called, them he also justified: and whom he justified, them he also glorified.

Romans 8:29, 30

And the work of righteousness shall be peace; and the effect of righteousness quietness and assurance for ever.

Isaiah 32:17

In righteousness shalt thou be established: thou shalt be far from oppression; for thou shalt not fear: and from terror; for it shall not come near thee.

Behold, they shall surely gather together, but not by me: whosoever shall gather together against thee shall fall for thy sake.

Behold, I have created the smith that bloweth the coals in the fire, and that bringeth forth an instrument for his work; and I have created the waster to destroy.

No weapon that is formed against thee shall prosper; and every tongue that shall rise against thee in judgment thou shalt condemn. This is the heritage of the servants of the Lord, and their righteousness is of me, saith the Lord.

Isaiah 54:14-17

For with the heart man believeth unto righteousness; and with the mouth confession is made unto salvation.

Romans 10:10

Deliverer

The spirit of the Lord God is upon me; because the Lord hath anointed me to preach good tidings unto the meek; he hath sent me to bind up the brokenhearted, to proclaim liberty to the captives, and the opening of the prison to them that are bound;

Isaiah 61:1

And ye shall know the truth, and the truth shall make you free.

If the Son therefore shall make you free, ye shall be free indeed.

John 8:32, 36

For the law of the Spirit of life in Christ Jesus hath made me free from the law of sin and death.

Romans 8:2

Now the Lord is that Spirit: and where the Spirit of the Lord is, there is Liberty.

II Corinthians 3:17

But now being made free from sin, and become servants to God, ye have your fruit unto holiness, and the end everlasting life.

Romans 6:22

For thou hast broken the yoke of his burden, and the staff of his shoulder, the rod of his oppressor, as in the day of Midian.

Isaiah 9:4

The Spirit of the Lord is upon me, because he hath anointed me to preach the gospel to the poor; he hath sent me to heal the brokenhearted, to preach deliverance to the captives, and recovering of sight to the blind, to set at liberty them that are bruised,

Luke 4:18

Behold, I give unto you power to tread on serpents and scorpions, and over all the power of the enemy: and nothing shall by any means hurt you.

Luke 10:19

And these signs shall follow them that believe; In my name shall they cast out devils; they shall speak with new tongues;

Mark 16:17

And they overcame him by the blood of the Lamb, and by the word of their testimony; and they loved not their lives unto the death.

Revelation 12:11

Beloved, believe not every spirit, but try the spirits whether they are of God: because many false prophets are gone out into the world.

Hereby know ye the Spirit of God: Every spirit that confesseth that Jesus Christ is come in the flesh is of God.

And every spirit that confesseth not that Jesus Christ is come in the flesh is not of God: and this is that spirit of antichrist, whereof ye have heard that it should come; and even now already is it in the world.

Ye are of God, little children, and have overcome them: because greater is he that is in you, than he that is in the world.

I John 4:1-4

JESUS IS YOUR
Fellowship

That which we have seen and heard declare we unto you, that ye also may have fellowship with us: and truly our fellowship is with the Father, and with his Son Jesus Christ.

I John 1:3

God is faithful, by whom ye were called unto the fellowship of his Son Jesus Christ our Lord.

I Corinthians 1:9

Behold, I stand at the door, and knock: if any man hear my voice, and open the door, I will come in to him, and will sup with him, and he with me.

Revelation 3:20

Jesus answered and said unto him, If a man love me, he will keep my words: and my Father will love him, and we will come unto him, and make our abode with him.

John 14:23

Sing and rejoice, O daughter of Zion: for, lo, I come, and I will dwell in the midst of thee, saith the Lord.

Zechariah 2:10

For where two or three are gathered together in my name, there am I in the midst of them.

Matthew 18:20

He that hath my commandments, and keepeth them, he it is that loveth me: and he that loveth me shall be loved of my Father, and I will love him, and will manifest myself to him.

John 14:21

Abide in me, and I in you. As the branch cannot bear fruit of itself, except it abide in the vine; no more can ye, except ye abide in me.

I am the vine, ye are the branches: He that abideth in me, and I in him, the same bringeth forth much fruit: for without me ye can do nothing.

If ye abide in me, and my words abide in you, ye shall ask what ye will, and it shall be done unto you.

John 15:4, 5, 7

If there be therefore any consolation in Christ, if any comfort of love, if any fellowship of the Spirit, if any bowels and mercies,

Fulfil ye my joy, that ye be likeminded, having the same love, being of one accord, of one mind.

Philippians 2:1, 2

I am a companion of all them that fear thee, and of them that keep thy precepts.

Psalm 119:63

And walk in love, as Christ also hath loved us, and hath given himself for us an offering and a sacrifice to God for a sweet-smelling savour.

Speaking to yourselves in psalms and hymns and spiritual songs, singing and making melody in your heart to the Lord;

For we are members of his body, of his flesh, and of his bones.

Ephesians 5:2, 19, 30

This then is the message which we have heard of him, and declare unto you, that God is light, and in him is no darkness at all.

If we say that we have fellowship with him, and walk in darkness, we lie, and do not the truth:

But if we walk in the light, as he is in the light, we have fellowship one with another, and the blood of Jesus Christ his Son cleanseth us from all sin.

1 John 1:5-7

JESUS IS YOUR
Example

For even hereunto were ye called: because Christ also suffered for us, leaving us an example, that ye should follow his steps:
I Peter 2:21

He that saith he abideth in him ought himself also so to walk, even as he walked.
I John 2:6

Be ye therefore followers of God, as dear Children:
And walk in love, as Christ also hath loved us, and hath given himself for us an offering and a sacrifice to God for a sweet-smelling savour.
Ephesians 5:1, 2

Let this mind be in you, which was also in Christ Jesus:
Who, being in the form of God, thought it not robbery to be equal with God:
But made himself of no reputation, and took upon him the form of a servant, and was made in the likeness of men:
And being found in fashion as a man, he humbled himself, and became obedient unto death, even the death of the cross.
Philippians 2:5-8

But so shall it not be among you: but whosoever will be great among you, shall be your minister:

And whosoever of you will be the chiefest, shall be servant of all.

For even the Son of man came not to be ministered unto, but to minister, and to give his life a ransom for many.

Mark 10:43-45

If I then, your Lord and Master, have washed your feet; ye also ought to wash one another's feet.

For I have given you an example, that ye should do as I have done to you.

John 13:14, 15

A new commandment I give unto you, That ye love one another; as I have loved you, that ye also love one another.

John 13:34

Hereby perceive we the love of God, because he laid down his life for us: and we ought to lay down our lives for the brethren.

I John 3:16

Now the God of patience and consolation grant you to be like-minded one toward another according to Christ Jesus:

That ye may with one mind and one mouth glorify God, even the Father of our Lord Jesus Christ.

Wherefore receive ye one another, as Christ also received us to the glory of God.

Romans 15:5-7

Forbearing one another, and forgiving one another, if any man have a quarrel against any: even as Christ forgave you, so also do ye.

Colossians 3:13

Looking unto Jesus the author and finisher of our faith; who for the joy that was set before him endured the cross, despising the shame, and is set down at the right hand of the throne of God.

For consider him that endured such contradiction of sinners against himself, lest ye be wearied and faint in your minds.

Hebrews 12:2, 3

Companion

I am a companion of all them that fear thee, and of them that keep thy precepts.

Psalm 119:63

A man that hath friends must shew himself friendly: and there is a friend that sticketh closer than a brother.

Proverbs 18:24

Let your conversation be without covetousness; and be content with such things as ye have: for he hath said, I will never leave thee, nor forsake thee.

Hebrews 13:5

Henceforth I call you not servants; for the servant knoweth not what his lord doeth: but I have called you friends; for all things that I have heard of my Father I have made known unto you.

Ye have not chosen me, but I have chosen you, and ordained you, that ye should go and bring forth fruit, and that your fruit should remain: that whatsoever ye shall ask of the Father in my name, he may give it you.

John 15:15, 16

But if we walk in the light, as he is in the light, we have fellowship one with another, and the blood of Jesus Christ his Son cleanseth us from all sin.

I John 1:7

For the mountains shall depart, and the hills be removed; but my kindness shall not depart from thee, neither shall the covenant of my peace be removed, saith the Lord that hath mercy on thee.

Isaiah 54:10

Behold, I stand at the door, and knock: if any man hear my voice, and open the door, I will come in to him, and will sup with him, and he with me.

Revelation 3:20

Draw nigh to God, and he will draw nigh to you. Cleanse your hands, ye sinners; and purify your hearts, ye double-minded.

James 4:8

When my father and my mother forsake me, then the Lord will take me up.

Psalm 27:10

This is my commandment, That ye love one another, as I have loved you.

Greater love hath no man than this, that a man lay down his life for his friends.

Ye are my friends, if you do whatsoever I command you.

John 15:12-14

God is faithful, by whom ye were called unto the fellowship of his Son Jesus Christ our Lord.

I Corinthians 1:9

That which we have seen and heard declare we unto you, that ye also may have fellowship with us: and truly our fellowship is with the Father, and with his Son Jesus Christ.

I John 1:3

I will not leave you comfortless: I will come to you.

John 14:18

Brother

For whosoever shall do the will of my Father which is in heaven, the same is my brother, and sister, and mother.

Matthew 12:50

For both he that sanctifieth and they who are sanctified are all of one: for which cause he is not ashamed to call them brethren,

Hebrews 2:11

For whom he did foreknow, he also did predestinate to be conformed to the image of his Son, that he might be the firstborn among many brethren.

Romans 8:29

For ye are all the children of God by faith in Christ Jesus.

Galatians 3:26

But as many as receive him, to them gave he power to become the sons of God, even to them that believe on his name:

John 1:12

Now therefore ye are no more strangers and foreigners, but fellow-citizens with the saints, and of the household of God;

Ephesians 2:19

Behold, what manner of love the Father hath bestowed upon us, that we should be called the sons of God: therefore the world knoweth us not, because it knew him not.

I John 3:1

And because ye are sons, God hath sent forth the Spirit of his Son into your hearts, crying Abba, Father.

Wherefore thou art no more a servant, but a son; and if a son, then an heir of God through Christ.

Galatians 4:6, 7

For as many as are led by the Spirit of God, they are the sons of God.

Romans 8:14

Beloved, now are we the sons of God, and it doth not yet appear what we shall be: but we know that, when he shall appear, we shall be like him; for we shall see him as he is.

I John 3:2

Guardian

When thou passest through the waters, I will be with thee; and through the rivers, they shall not overflow thee: when thou walkest through the fire, thou shalt not be burned; neither shall the flame kindle upon thee.

Isaiah 43:2

But thou, O Lord, art a shield for me; my glory, and the lifter up of mine head.

Psalm 3:3

For the eyes of the Lord run to and fro throughout the whole earth, to shew himself strong in the behalf of them whose heart is perfect toward him.

II Chronicles 16:9a

The Lord your God which goeth before you, he shall fight for you, according to all that he did for you in Egypt before your eyes;

Deuteronomy 1:30

But the Lord is faithful, who shall stablish you, and keep you from evil.

II Thessalonians 3:3

But if thou shalt indeed obey his voice, and do all that I speak; then I will be an enemy unto thine enemies, and an adversary unto thine adversaries.

Exodus 23:22

He will keep the feet of his saints, and the wicked shall be silent in darkness; for by strength shall no man prevail.

I Samuel 2:9

For thou hast been a shelter for me, and a strong tower from the enemy.

Psalm 61:3

The Lord thy God in the midst of thee is mighty; he will save, he will rejoice over thee with joy; he will rest in his love, he will joy over thee with singing.

Zephaniah 3:17

For the eyes of the Lord are over the righteous, and his ears are open unto their prayers: but the face of the Lord is against them that do evil.

And who is he that will harm you, if ye be followers of that which is good?

I Peter 3:12, 13

The eternal God is thy refuge, underneath are the everlasting arms: and he shall thrust out the enemy from before thee; and shall say, Destroy them.

Deuteronomy 33:27

A thousand shall fall at thy side, and ten thousand at thy right hand; but it shall not come nigh thee.

Psalm 91:7

So shall they fear the name of the Lord from the west, and his glory from the rising of the sun. When the enemy shall come in like a flood, the Spirit of the Lord shall lift up a standard against him.

Isaiah 59:19

Security

Blessed be the God and Father of our Lord Jesus Christ, which according to his abundant mercy hath begotten us again unto a lively hope by the resurrection of Jesus Christ from the dead,

To an inheritance incorruptible, and undefiled, and that fadeth not away, reserved in heaven for you,

Who are kept by the power of God through faith unto salvation ready to be revealed in the last time.

I Peter 1:3-5

My sheep hear my voice, and I know them, and they follow me:

And I give unto them eternal life; and they shall never perish, neither shall any man pluck them out of my hand.

My Father, which gave them me, is greater than all; and no man is able to pluck them out of my Father's hand.

John 10:27-29

For I am persuaded, that neither death, nor life, nor angels, nor principalities, nor powers, nor things present, nor things to come,

Nor height, nor depth, nor any other creature, shall be able to separate us from the love of God, which is in Christ Jesus our Lord.

Romans 8:38, 39

Being confident of this very thing, that he which hath begun a good work in you will perform it until the day of Jesus Christ:

Philippians 1:6

But the Lord is faithful, who shall stablish you, and keep you from evil.

II Thessalonians 3:3

All that the Father giveth me shall come to me; and him that cometh to me I will in no wise cast out.

John 6:37

Now unto him that is able to keep you from falling, and to present you faultless before the presence of his glory with exceeding joy,

To the only wise God our Saviour, be glory and majesty, dominion and power, both now and ever. Amen.

Jude 24, 25

Lift up your eyes on high, and behold who hath created these things, that bringeth out their host by number: he calleth them all by names by the greatness of his might, for that he is strong in power; not one faileth.

Isaiah 40:26

Surely goodness and mercy shall follow me all the days of my life: and I will dwell in the house of the Lord for ever.

Psalm 23:6

Labour not for the meat which perisheth, but for that meat which endureth unto everlasting life, which the Son of man shall give unto you: for him hath God the Father sealed.

John 6:27

Who hath also sealed us, and given the earnest of the Spirit in our hearts.

II Corinthians 1:22

In whom ye also trusted, after that ye heard the word of truth, the gospel of your salvation: in whom also after that ye believed, ye were sealed with that holy Spirit of promise,

Ephesians 1:13

And grieve not the holy Spirit of God, whereby ye are sealed unto the day of redemption.

Ephesians 4:30

And we desire that every one of you do shew the same diligence to the full assurance of hope unto the end:

That ye be not slothful, but followers of them who through faith and patience inherit the promises.

That by two immutable things, in which it was impossible for God to lie, we might have a strong consolation, who have fled for refuge to lay hold upon the hope set before us:

Which hope we have as an anchor of the soul, both sure and stedfast, and which entereth into that within the veil;

Whither the forerunner is for us entered, even Jesus, made an high priest for ever after the order of Melchisedec.

Hebrews 6:11, 12, 18-20

Sufficiency

And God is able to make all grace abound toward you; that ye, always having all sufficiency in all things, may abound to every good work:

II Corinthians 9:8

But my God shall supply all your need according to his riches in glory by Christ Jesus.

Philippians 4:19

Therefore I say unto you, What things soever ye desire, when ye pray, believe that ye receive them, and ye shall have them.

Mark 11:24

Not that we are sufficient of ourselves to think any thing as of ourselves; but our sufficiency is of God;

II Corinthians 3:5

I can do all things through Christ which strengtheneth me.

Philippians 4:13

And what is the exceeding greatness of his power to us-ward who believe, according to the working of his mighty power,

Ephesians 1:19

And he said unto me, My grace is sufficient for thee: for my strength is made perfect in weakness. Most gladly therefore will I rather glory in my infirmities, that the power of Christ may rest upon me.

II Corinthians 12:9

Nay, in all these things we are more than conquerors through him that loved us.

Romans 8:37

Blessed by the God and Father of our Lord Jesus Christ, who hath blessed us with all spiritual blessings in heavenly places in Christ:

Ephesians 1:3

If ye abide in me, and my words abide in you, ye shall ask what ye will, and it shall be done unto you.

John 15:7

And whatsoever ye shall ask in my name, that will I do, that the Father may be glorified in the Son.

John 14:13

And in that day ye shall ask me nothing. Verily, verily, I say unto you, Whatsoever ye shall ask the Father in my name, he will give it you.

John 16:23, 24

And all things, whatsoever ye shall ask in prayer, believing, ye shall receive.

Matthew 21:22

He that spared not his own Son, but delivered him up for us all, how shall he not with him also freely give us all things?

Romans 8:32

According as his divine power hath given unto us all things that pertain unto life and godliness, through the knowledge of him that hath called us to glory and virtue:

Whereby are given unto us exceeding great and precious promises: that by these ye might be partakers of the divine nature, having escaped the corruption that is in the world through lust.

II Peter 1:3, 4

Bless the Lord, O my soul, and forget not all his benefits:

Who forgiveth all thine iniquities; who healeth all thy diseases;

Who redeemeth thy life from destruction; who crowneth thee with lovingkindness and tender mercies;

Psalm 103:2-4

Fulfillment

Blessed are they which do hunger and thirst after righteousness: for they shall be filled.

Matthew 5:6

Delight thyself also in the Lord; and he shall give thee the desires of thine heart.

Psalm 37:4

For he satisfieth the longing soul, and filleth the hungry soul with goodness.

Psalm 107:9

Who satisfieth thy mouth with good things; so that thy youth is renewed like the eagle's.

Psalm 103:5

And ye shall eat in plenty, and be satisfied, and praise the name of the Lord your God, that hath dealt wondrously with you: and my people shall never be ashamed.

Joel 2:26

And Jesus said unto them, I am the bread of life: he that cometh to me shall never hunger; and he that believeth on me shall never thirst.

John 6:35

The meek shall eat and be satisfied: they shall praise the Lord that seek him: your heart shall live for ever.

Psalm 22:26

Jesus answered and said unto her, Whosoever drinketh of this water shall thirst again:

But whosoever drinketh of the water that I shall give him shall never thirst; but the water that I shall give him shall be in him a well of water springing up into everlasting life.

John 4:13, 14

Yea, the Lord will answer and say unto his people, Behold, I will send you corn, and wine, and oil, and ye shall be satisfied therewith: and I will no more make you a reproach among the heathen:

Joel 2:19

And if thou draw out thy soul to the hungry, and satisfy the afflicted soul; then shall thy light rise in obscurity, and thy darkness be as the noon day: And the Lord shall guide thee continually, and satisfy thy soul in drought, and make fat thy bones: and thou shalt be like a watered garden, and like a spring of water, whose waters fail not.

Isaiah 58:10, 11

The eyes of all wait upon thee; and thou givest them their meat in due season.

Thou openest thine hand, and satisfiest the desire of every living thing.

Psalm 145:15, 16

Wherefore do ye spend money for that which is not bread? and your labour for that which satisfieth not? hearken diligently unto me, and eat ye that which is good, and let your soul delight itself in fatness.

Isaiah 55:2

And I will satiate the soul of the priests with fatness, and my people shall be satisfied with my goodness, saith the Lord.

Jeremiah 31:14

My soul shall be satisfied as with marrow and fatness; and my mouth shall praise thee with joyful lips:

When I remember thee upon my bed, and meditate on thee in the night watches.

Psalm 63:5, 6

He that spared not his own Son, but delivered him up for us all, how shall he not with him also freely give us all things?

Romans 8:32

JESUS IS YOUR
Everything

But my God shall supply all your need according to his riches in glory by Christ Jesus.

Philippians 4:19

I can do all things through Christ which strengtheneth me.

Philippians 4:13

Nay, in all these things we are more than conquerors through him that loved us.

Romans 8:37

Therefore let no man glory in men. For all things are yours;

Whether Paul, or Apollos, or Cephas, or the world, or life, or death, or things present, or things to come; all are yours;

And ye are Christ's and Christ is God's.

I Corinthians 3:21-23

If ye abide in me, and my words abide in you, ye shall ask what ye will, and it shall be done unto you.

John 15:7

And in that day ye shall ask me nothing. Verily, verily, I say unto you, Whatsoever ye shall ask the Father in my name, he will give it you.

Hitherto have ye asked nothing in my name: ask and ye shall receive, that your joy may be full.

John 16:23, 24

And all things, whatsoever ye shall ask in prayer, believing, ye shall receive.

Matthew 21:22

Therefore I say unto you, What things soever ye desire, when ye pray, believe that ye receive them, and ye shall have them.

Mark 11:24

Blessed be the God and Father of our Lord Jesus Christ, who hath blessed us with all spiritual blessings in heavenly places in Christ.

Ephesians 1:3

And whatsoever we ask, we receive of him, because we keep his commandments, and do those things that are pleasing in his sight.

I John 3:22

For he hath made him to be sin for us, who knew no sin; that we might be made the righteousness of God in him.

II Corinthians 5:21

For to me to live is Christ, and to die is gain.

Philippians 1:21

Therefore if any man be in Christ, he is a new creature: old things are passed away; behold, all things are become new.

II Corinthians 5:17

Now unto him that is able to do exceeding abundantly above all that we ask or think, according to the power that worketh in us,

Unto him be glory in the church by Christ Jesus throughout all ages, world without end. Amen.

Ephesians 3:20, 21

And God is able to make all grace abound toward you; that ye, always having all sufficiency in all things, may abound to every good work:

II Corinthians 9:8

Blessed be the Lord, who daily loadeth us with benefits, even the God of our salvation. Selah.

Psalm 68:19

The Bible Is Your. . .

THE BIBLE IS YOUR

Infallible Authority

All Scripture is given by inspiration of God, and is profitable for doctrine, for reproof, for correction, for instruction in righteousness.

II Timothy 3:16

Knowing this first, that no prophecy of the scripture is of any private interpretation.
For the prophecy came not in old time by the will of man: but holy men of God spake as they were moved by the Holy Ghost.
II Peter 1:20, 21

For the word of God is quick, and powerful, and sharper than any two-edged sword, piercing even to the dividing asunder of soul and spirit, and of the joints and marrow, and is a discerner of the thoughts and intents of the heart.

Hebrews 4:12

For as the rain cometh down, and the snow from heaven, and returneth not thither, but watereth the earth, and maketh it bring forth and bud, that it may give seed to the sower, and bread to the eater:
So shall my word be that goeth forth out of my mouth: it shall not return unto me

void, but it shall accomplish that which I please, and it shall prosper in the thing whereto I sent it.

Isaiah 55:10, 11

Search the scriptures; for in them ye think ye have eternal life: and they are they which testify of me.

John 5:39

Being born again, not of corruptible seed, but of incorruptible, by the word of God, which liveth and abideth for ever.

I Peter 1:23

For he spake, and it was done; he commanded, and it stood fast.

Psalm 33:9

Every word of God is pure: he is a shield unto them that put their trust in him.

Proverbs 30:5

For ever, O Lord, thy word is settled in heaven.

Psalm 119:89

By the word of the Lord were the heavens made; and all the host of them by the breath of his mouth.

Psalm 33:6

For all the promises of God in him are yea, and in him Amen, unto the glory of God by us.

II Corinthians 1:20

For all flesh is as grass, and all the glory of man as the flower of grass. The grass withereth, and the flower thereof falleth away:

But the word of the Lord endureth for ever. And this is the word which by the gospel is preached unto you.

I Peter 1:24, 25

Heaven and earth shall pass away: but my words shall not pass away.

Mark 13:31

THE BIBLE IS YOUR
Deed of Inheritance

And now, brethren, I commend you to God, and to the word of his grace, which is able to build you up, and to give you an inheritance among all them which are sanctified.

Acts 20:32

To open their eyes, and to turn them from darkness to light, and from the power of Satan unto God, that they may receive forgiveness of sins, and inheritance among them which are sanctified by faith that is in me.

Acts 26:18

The Spirit itself beareth witness with our spirit, that we are the children of God:

And if children, then heirs; heirs of God, and joint-heirs with Christ; if so be that we suffer with him, that we may be also glorified together.

Romans 8:16, 17

In whom also we have obtained an inheritance, being predestinated according to the purpose of him who worketh all things after the counsel of his own will:

That we should be to the praise of his glory, who first trusted in Christ.

In whom ye also trusted, after that ye heard the word of truth, the gospel of your salvation: in whom also after that ye believed, ye were sealed with the holy Spirit of promise,

Which is the earnest of our inheritance until the redemption of the purchased possession, unto the praise of his glory.

Ephesians 1:11-14

And if ye be Christ's then are ye Abraham's seed, and heirs according to the promise.

Galatians 3:29

That the Gentiles should be fellow-heirs, and of the same body and partakers of his promise in Christ by the gospel:

Ephesians 3:6

In my Father's house are many mansions: if it were not so, I would have told you. I go to prepare a place for you.

And if I go and prepare a place for you, I will come again, and receive you unto myself; that where I am, there ye may be also.

John 14:2, 3

But now they desire a better country, that is, an heavenly: wherefore God is not ashamed to be called their God: for he hath prepared for them a city.

Hebrews 11:16

Then shall the King say unto them on his right hand, Come, ye blessed of my Father, inherit the kingdom prepared for you from the foundation of the world:

Matthew 25:34

For all the promises of God in him are yea, and in him Amen, unto the glory of God by us.

II Corinthians 1:20

Blessed be the God and Father of our Lord Jesus Christ, which according to his abundant mercy hath begotten us again unto a lively hope by the resurrection of Jesus Christ from the dead,

To an inheritance incorruptible, and undefiled, and that fadeth not away, reserved in heaven for you,

I Peter 1:3, 4

But as it is written, Eye hath not seen, nor ear heard, neither have entered into the heart of man, the things which God hath prepared for them that love him.

I Corinthians 2:9

Whereby are given unto us exceeding great and precious promises: that by these ye might be partakers of the divine nature, having escaped the corruption that is in the world through lust.

II Peter 1:4

And whatsoever ye do, do it heartily,
as to the Lord, and not unto men;

Knowing that of the Lord ye shall
receive the reward of the inheritance: for ye
serve the Lord Christ.

Colossians 3:23, 24

Wait on the Lord, and keep his way,
and he shall exalt thee to inherit the land:
when the wicked are cut off, thou shalt see
it.

Psalm 37:34

Guide for Life

Thy word is a lamp unto my feet, and a light unto my path.

Psalm 119:105

When thou goest, it shall lead thee; when thou sleepest, it shall keep thee; and when thou awakest, it shall talk with thee.
For the commandment is a lamp and the law is light; and reproofs of instruction are the way of life:

Proverbs 6:22, 23

Thy word have I hid in mine heart, that I might not sin against thee.

Psalm 119:11

Moreover by them is thy servant warned; and in keeping of them there is great reward.

Psalm 19:11

Wherewithal shall a young man cleanse his way? by taking heed thereto according to thy word.

Psalm 119:9

Then said Jesus to those Jews which believed on him, if ye continue in my word, then are ye my disciples indeed;

And ye shall know the truth, and the truth shall make you free.

John 8:31, 32

Thy testimonies also are my delight and my counsellors.

Psalm 119:24

Whereby are given unto us exceeding great and precious promises: that by these ye might be partakers of the divine nature, having escaped the corruption that is in the world through lust.

II Peter 1:4

The steps of a good man are ordered by the Lord: and he delighteth in his way.

Psalm 37:23

I will instruct thee and teach thee in the way which thou shalt go: I will guide thee with mine eye.

Psalm 32:8

He restoreth my soul: he leadeth me in the paths of righteousness for his name's sake.

Psalm 23:3

And thine ears shall hear a word behind thee, saying, This is the way, walk ye in it, when ye turn to the right hand, and when ye turn to the left.

Isaiah 30:21

As he spake by the mouth of his holy prophets, which have been since the world began.

To give light to them that sit in darkness and in the shadow of death, to guide our feet into the way of peace.

Luke 1:70, 79

This book of the law shall not depart out of thy mouth; but thou shalt meditate therein day and night, that thou mayest observe to do according to all that is written therein: for then thou shalt make thy way prosperous, and then thou shalt have good success.

Joshua 1:8

All scripture is given by inspiration of God, and is profitable for doctrine, for reproof, for correction, for instruction in righteousness:

That the man of God may be perfect, throughly furnished unto all good works.

II Timothy 3:16, 17

Stability

Being born again, not of corruptible seed, but of incorruptible, by the word of God, which liveth and abideth for ever.

For all flesh is as grass, and all the glory of man as the flower of grass. The grass withereth, and the flower thereof falleth away:

But the word of the Lord endureth for ever. And this is the word which by the gospel is preached unto you.

I Peter 1:23-25

Heaven and earth shall pass away, but my words shall not pass away.

Matthew 24:35

For ever, O Lord, thy word is settled in heaven.

Psalm 119:89

The grass withereth, the flower fadeth: but the word of our God shall stand for ever.

Isaiah 40:8

For verily I say unto you, Till heaven and earth pass, one jot or one tittle shall in no wise pass from the law, till all be fulfilled.

Matthew 5:18

Blessed be the Lord, that hath given rest unto his people Israel, according to all that he promised: there hath not failed one word of all his good promise,

I Kings 8:56a

For I am the Lord: I will speak, and the word that I shall speak shall come to pass; it shall be no more prolonged: for in your days, O rebellious house, will I say the word, and will perform it, saith the Lord God.

Ezekiel 12:25

My son, attend to my words; incline thine ear unto my sayings.

Let them not depart from thine eyes; keep them in the midst of thine heart.

For they are life unto those that find them, and health to all their flesh.

Proverbs 4:20-22

What shall we then say to these things? If God be for us, who can be against us?

Romans 8:31

The eternal God is thy refuge, and underneath are the everlasting arms: and he shall thrust out the enemy from before thee; and shall say, Destroy them.

Deuteronomy 33:27

He brought me up also out of an horrible pit, out of the miry clay, and set my feet upon a rock, and established my goings.

Psalm 40:2

God is our refuge and strength, a very present help in trouble.

Psalm 46:1

The name of the Lord is a strong tower: the righteous runneth into it, and is safe.

Proverbs 18:10

But the Lord is faithful, who shall stablish you, and keep you from evil.

II Thessalonians 3:3

Now unto him that is able to keep you from falling, and to present you faultless before the presence of his glory with exceeding joy,

To the only wise God our Saviour, be glory and majesty, dominion and power, both now and ever. Amen.

Jude 24, 25

Strength

O man greatly beloved, fear not: peace be unto thee, be strong, yea, be strong. And when he had spoken unto me, I was strengthened, and said, Let my lord speak; for thou hast strengthened me.

Daniel 10:19

My soul melteth for heaviness: strengthen thou me according unto thy word.

Psalm 119:28

For thus saith the Lord God, the Holy One of Israel; In returning and rest shall ye be saved; in quietness and in confidence shall be your strength:

Isaiah 30:15

That he would grant you, according to the riches of his glory, to be strengthened with might by his Spirit in the inner man;

That Christ may dwell in your hearts by faith; that ye, being rooted and grounded in love,

Ephesians 3:16, 17

That ye might walk worthy of the Lord unto all pleasing, being fruitful in every good work, and increasing in the knowledge of God.

Strengthened with all might, according to his glorious power, unto all patience and longsuffering with joyfulness;

Giving thanks unto the Father, which hath made us meet to be partakers of the inheritance of the saints in light:

Colossians 1:10-12

But they that wait upon the Lord shall renew their strength; they shall mount up with wings as eagles; they shall run, and not be weary; and they shall walk, and not faint.

Isaiah 40:31

Then he said unto them, Go your way, eat the fat, and drink the sweet, and send portions unto them for whom nothing is prepared: for this day is holy unto our Lord: neither be ye sorry; for the joy of the Lord is your strength.

Nehemiah 8:10

I can do all things through Christ which strengtheneth me.

Philippians 4:13

Fear thou not; for I am with thee: be not dismayed; for I am thy God: I will strengthen thee; yea, I will help thee; yea, I will uphold thee with the right hand of my righteousness.

Isaiah 41:10

Counsel is mine, and sound wisdom: I am understanding; I have strength.

Proverbs 8:14

He giveth power to the faint; and to them that have no might he increaseth strength.

Isaiah 40:29

The Lord is my rock, and my fortress, and my deliverer; my God, my strength, in whom I will trust; my buckler, and the horn of my salvation, and my high tower.

Psalm 18:2

Wherefore take unto you the whole armour of God, that ye may be able to withstand in the evil day, and having done all, to stand.

Ephesians 6:13

The Lord is my light and my salvation; whom shall I fear? the Lord is the strength of my life; of whom shall I be afraid?

Psalm 27:1

Finally, my brethren, be strong in the Lord, and in the power of his might.

Ephesians 6:10

What To Do When
You Feel . . .

Discouraged

Therefore the redeemed of the Lord shall return, and come with singing unto Zion; and everlasting joy shall be upon their head: they shall obtain gladness and joy; and sorrow and mourning shall flee away.

Isaiah 51:11

Wherein ye greatly rejoice, though now for a season, if need be, ye are in heaviness through manifold temptations:

That the trial of your faith, being much more precious than of gold that perisheth, though it be tried with fire, might be found unto praise and honour and glory at the appearing of Jesus Christ:

Whom having not seen, ye love; in whom, though now ye see him not, yet believing, ye rejoice with joy unspeakable and full of glory:

Receiving the end of your faith, even the salvation of your souls.

I Peter 1:6-9

Be careful for nothing: but in every thing by prayer and supplication with thanksgiving let your requests be made known unto God.

And the peace of God, which passeth all understanding, shall keep your hearts and minds through Christ Jesus.

Finally, brethren, whatsoever things are true, whatsoever things are honest, whatsoever things are just, whatsoever things are pure, whatsoever things are lovely, whatsoever things are of good report; if there be any virtue, and if there be any praise, think on these things.

Philippians 4:6-8

Though I walk in the midst of trouble, thou wilt revive me: thou shalt stretch forth thine hand against the wrath of mine enemies, and thy right hand shall save me.

Psalm 138:7

Let not your heart be troubled: ye believe in God, believe also in me.

John 14:1

Peace, I leave with you, my peace I give unto you: not as the world giveth, give I unto you. Let not your heart be troubled, neither let it be afraid.

John 14:27

We are troubled on every side, yet not distressed; we are perplexed, but not in despair;

Persecuted, but not forsaken; cast down, but not destroyed;

II Corinthians 4:8, 9

Cast not away therefore your confidence, which hath great recompence of reward.

For ye have need of patience, that, after ye have done the will of God, ye might receive the promise.

Hebrews 10:35, 36

Being confident of this very thing, that he which hath begun a good work in you will perform it until the day of Jesus Christ:

Philippians 1:6

And let us not be weary in well doing: for in due season we shall reap, if we faint not.

Galatians 6:9

Be of good courage, and he shall strengthen your heart, all ye that hope in the Lord.

Psalm 31:24

The Lord is my light and my salvation; whom shall I fear? the Lord is the strength of my life; of whom shall I be afraid?

When the wicked, even mine enemies and my foes, came upon me to eat up my flesh, they stumbled and fell.

Though an host shall encamp against me, my heart shall not fear: though war should rise against me, in this will I be confident.

One thing have I desired of the Lord, that will I seek after; that I may dwell in the house of the Lord all the days of my life, to behold the beauty of the Lord, and to enquire in his temple.

For in the time of trouble he shall hide me in his pavilion: in the secret of his tabernacle shall he hide me; he shall set me up upon a rock.

And now shall mine head be lifted up above mine enemies round about me: therefore will I offer in his tabernacle sacrifices of joy; I will sing, yea, I will sing praises unto the Lord.

Hear, O Lord, when I cry with my voice: have mercy also upon me, and answer me.

When thou saidst, Seek ye my face; my heart said unto thee, Thy face, Lord, will I seek.

Hide not thy face far from me; put not thy servant away in anger: thou hast been my help; leave me not, neither forsake me, O God of my salvation.

When my father and my mother forsake me, then the Lord will take me up.

Teach me thy way, O Lord, and lead me in a plain path, because of mine enemies.

Deliver me not over unto the will of mine enemies: for false witnesses are risen up against me, and such as breathe out cruelty:

I had fainted, unless I had believed to see the goodness of the Lord in the land of the living.

Wait on the Lord: be of good courage, and he shall strengthen thine heart: wait, I say, on the Lord.

Psalm 27:1-14

Worried

Casting all your care upon him; for he careth for you.

I Peter 5:7

Let not your heart be troubled: ye believe in God, believe also in me.

John 14:1

Be careful for nothing; but in every thing by prayer and supplication with thanksgiving let your requests be made known unto God.

And the peace of God, which passeth all understanding, shall keep your hearts and minds through Christ Jesus.

Philippians 4:6, 7

And let the peace of God rule in your hearts, to the which also ye are called in one body; and be ye thankful.

Colossians 3:15

Thou wilt keep him in perfect peace, whose mind is stayed on thee: because he trusteth in thee.

Isaiah 26:3

I will both lay me down in peace, and sleep: for thou, Lord, only makest me dwell in safety.

Psalm 4:8

But my God shall supply all your need according to his riches in glory by Christ Jesus.

Philippians 4:19

Therefore I say unto you, Take no thought for your life, what ye shall eat, or what ye shall drink; nor yet for your body, what ye shall put on. Is not the life more than meat, and the body than raiment?

Behold the fowls of the air: for they sow not, neither do they reap, nor gather into barns; yet your heavenly Father feedeth them. Are ye not much better than they?

Which of you by taking thought can add one cubit unto his stature?

And why take ye thought for raiment? Consider the lilies of the field, how they grow; they toil not, neither do they spin:

And yet I say unto you, That even Solomon in all his glory was not arrayed like one of these.

Wherefore, if God so clothe the grass of the field, which today is, and to-morrow is cast into the oven, shall he not much more clothe you, O ye of little faith?

Therefore take no thought, saying, What shall we eat? or, What shall we drink? or, Wherewithal shall we be clothed?

(For after all these things do the Gentiles seek:) for your heavenly Father knoweth that ye have need of all these things.

But seek ye first the kingdom of God, and his righteousness; and all these things shall be added unto you.

Take therefore no thought for the morrow: for the morrow shall take thought for the things of itself. Sufficient unto the day is the evil thereof.

Matthew 6:25-34

For to be carnally minded is death; but to be spiritually minded is life and peace.

Romans 8:6

When thou liest down, thou shalt not be afraid: yea, thou shalt lie down, and thy sleep shall be sweet.

Proverbs 3:24

For we which have believed do enter into rest, as he said, As I have sworn in my wrath, if they shall enter into my rest: although the works were finished from the foundation of the world,

There remaineth therefore a rest to the people of God.

Hebrews 4:3, 9

Great peace have they which love thy
law: and nothing shall offend them.

Psalm 119:165

He that dwelleth in the secret place of
the most High shall abide under the shadow
of the Almighty.

I will say of the Lord, He is my refuge
and my fortress: my God; in him will I trust.

Psalm 91:1, 2

Peace I leave with you, my peace I give
unto you: not as the world giveth, give I unto
you. Let not your heart be troubled, neither
let it be afraid.

John 14:27

WHAT TO DO WHEN YOU FEEL

Lonely

Let your conversation be without covetousness; and be content with such things as ye have: for he hath said, I will never leave thee, nor forsake thee.

Hebrews 13:5

Teaching them to observe all things whatsoever I have commanded you: and, lo, I am with you alway, even unto the end of the world. Amen.

Matthew 28:20

For the Lord will not forsake his people for his great name's sake: because it hath pleased the Lord to make you his people.

I Samuel 12:22

Fear thou not; for I am with thee: be not dismayed; for I am thy God: I will strengthen thee; yea, I will help thee; yea, I will uphold thee with the right hand of my righteousness.

Isaiah 41:10

I will not leave you comfortless: I will come to you.

John 14:18

Let not your heart be troubled: ye believe in God, believe also in me.

John 14:1

The eternal God is thy refuge, and underneath are the everlasting arms: and he shall thrust out the enemy from before thee; and shall say, Destroy them.

Deuteronomy 33:27

He healeth the broken in heart, and bindeth up their wounds.

Psalm 147:3

Who shall separate us from the love of Christ? shall tribulation, or distress, or persecution, or famine, or nakedness, or peril, or sword?

As it is written, For thy sake we are killed all the day long; we are accounted as sheep for the slaughter.

Nay, in all these things we are more than conquerers through him that loved us.

For I am persuaded, that neither death, nor life, nor angels, nor principalities, nor powers, nor things present, nor things to come,

Nor height, nor depth, nor any other creature, shall be able to separate us from the love of God, which is in Christ Jesus our Lord.

Romans 8:35-39

(For the Lord thy God is a merciful God;) he will not forsake thee, neither destroy thee, nor forget the covenant of thy fathers which he sware unto them.

Deuteronomy 4:31

Be strong and of a good courage, fear not, nor be afraid of them: for the Lord thy God, he it is that doth go with thee; he will not fail thee, nor forsake thee.

Deuteronomy 31:6

When my father and my mother forsake me, then the Lord will take me up.

Psalm 27:10

For the mountains shall depart, and the hills be removed; but my kindness shall not depart from thee, neither shall the covenant of my peace be removed, saith the Lord that hath mercy on thee.

Isaiah 54:10

Casting all your care upon him; for he careth for you.

I Peter 5:7

God is our refuge and strength, a very present help in trouble.

Psalm 46:1

WHAT TO DO WHEN YOU FEEL
Depressed

The righteous cry, and the Lord heareth, and delivereth them out of all their troubles.

Psalm 34:17

When thou passest through the waters, I will be with thee; and through the rivers, they shall not overflow thee: when thou walkest through the fire, thou shalt not be burned; neither shall the flame kindle upon thee.

Isaiah 43:2

For his anger endureth but a moment; in his favour is life: weeping may endure for a night, but joy cometh in the morning.

Psalm 30:5

Beloved, think it not strange concerning the fiery trial which is to try you, as though some strange thing happened unto you:

But rejoice, inasmuch as ye are partakers of Christ's sufferings; that, when his glory shall be revealed, ye may be glad also with exceeding joy.

I Peter 4:12, 13

To appoint unto them that mourn in Zion, to give unto them beauty for ashes, the oil of joy for mourning, the garment of praise for the spirit of heaviness; that they might be called trees of righteousness, the planting of the Lord, that he might be glorified.

Isaiah 61:3

But they that wait upon the Lord shall renew their strength; they shall mount up with wings as eagles; they shall run, and not be weary; and they shall walk, and not faint.

Isaiah 40:31

Blessed be God, even the Father of our Lord Jesus Christ, the Father of mercies, and the God of all comfort;

Who comforteth us in all our tribulation, that we may be able to comfort them which are in any trouble, by the comfort wherewith we ourselves are comforted of God.

II Corinthians 1:3, 4

For I am persuaded, that neither death, nor life, nor angels, nor principalities, nor powers, nor things present, nor things to come,

Nor height, nor depth, nor any other creature, shall be able to separate us from the love of God, which is in Christ Jesus our Lord.

Romans 8:38, 39

Finally, brethren, whatsoever things are true, whatsoever things are honest, whatsoever things are just, whatsoever things are pure, whatsoever things are lovely, whatsoever things are of good report; if there be any virtue, and if there be any praise, think on these things.

Philippians 4:8

He healeth the broken in heart, and bindeth up their wounds.

Psalm 147:3

Fear thou not; for I am with thee; be not dismayed; for I am thy God: I will strengthen thee; yea, I will help thee; yea, I will uphold thee with the right hand of my righteousness.

Isaiah 41:10

Humble yourselves therefore under the mighty hand of God, that he may exalt you in due time:

Casting all your care upon him; for he careth for you.

I Peter 5:6, 7

And he spake a parable unto them to this end, that men ought always to pray, and not to faint;

Luke 18:1

Then he said unto them, Go your way, eat the fat, and drink the sweet, and send portions unto them for whom nothing is prepared: for this day is holy unto our Lord: neither be ye sorry; for the joy of the Lord is your strength.

Nehemiah 8:10

Therefore the redeemed of the Lord shall return, and come with singing unto Zion; and everlasting joy shall be upon their head: they shall obtain gladness and joy; and sorrow and mourning shall flee away.

Isaiah 51:11

Dissatisfied

The young lions do lack, and suffer hunger: but they that seek the Lord shall not want any good thing.

Psalm 34:10

For I will pour water upon him that is thirsty, and floods upon the dry ground: I will pour my spirit upon thy seed, and my blessing upon thine offspring:

Isaiah 44:3

Trust in the Lord, and do good; so shalt thou dwell in the land, and verily thou shalt be fed.

Psalm 37:3

I know both how to be abased, and I know how to abound: every where and in all things I am instructed both to be full and to be hungry, both to abound and to suffer need.

I can do all things through Christ which strengtheneth me.

Philippians 4:12, 13

O God, thou art my God; early will I seek thee: my soul thirsteth for thee, my flesh longeth for thee in a dry and thirsty land, where no water is;

To see thy power and thy glory, so as I have seen thee in the sanctuary.

Because thy lovingkindness is better than life, my lips shall praise thee.

Thus will I bless thee while I live: I will lift up my hands in thy name.

My soul shall be satisfied as with marrow and fatness; and my mouth shall praise thee with joyful lips:

Psalm 63:1-5

A man shall be satisfied with good by the fruit of his mouth: and the recompence of a man's hands shall be rendered unto him.

Proverbs 12:14

And my people shall be satisfied with my goodness, saith the Lord.

Jeremiah 31:14b

And ye shall eat in plenty, and be satisfied, and praise the name of the Lord your God, that hath dealt wondrously with you: and my people shall never be ashamed.

Joel 2:26

Bless the lord, O my soul: and all that is within me, bless his holy name.

Bless the Lord, O my soul, and forget not all his benefits:

Who forgiveth all thine iniquities; who healeth all thy diseases;

Who redeemeth thy life from destruction; who crowneth thee with lovingkindness and tender mercies;

Who satisfieth thy mouth with good things; so that thy youth is renewed like the eagle's

Psalm 103:1-5

For he satisfieth the longing soul, and filleth the hungry soul with goodness.

Psalm 107:9

Behold, God is my salvation; I will trust, and not be afraid: for the Lord JEHOVAH is my strength and my song; he also is become my salvation.

Therefore with joy shall ye draw water out of the wells of salvation.

Isaiah 12:2, 3

And God is able to make all grace abound toward you; that ye, always having all sufficiency in all things, may abound to every good work:

II Corinthians 9:8

Ho, every one that thirsteth, come ye to the waters, and he that hath no money; come ye, buy, and eat; yea, come, buy wine and milk without money and without price.

Isaiah 55:1

Blessed are they which do hunger and thirst after righteousness: for they shall be filled.

Matthew 5:6

WHAT TO DO WHEN YOU FEEL
Condemned

There is therefore now no condemnation to them which are in Christ Jesus, who walk not after the flesh, but after the Spirit.

Romans 8:1

He hath not dealt with us after our sins; nor rewarded us according to our iniquities.

As far as the east is from the west, so far hath he removed our transgression from us.

Psalm 103:10, 12

Therefore if any man be in Christ, he is a new creature; old things are passed away; behold, all things are become new.

II Corinthians 5:17

For God sent not his Son into the world to condemn the world; but that the world through him might be saved.

He that believeth on him is not condemned: but he that believeth not is condemned already, because he hath not believed in the name of the only begotten Son of God.

John 3:17, 18

Verily, verily, I say unto you, He that heareth my word, and believeth on him that sent me, hath everlasting life, and shall not come into condemnation; but is passed from death unto life.

John 5:24

For I will be merciful to their unrighteousness, and their sins and their iniquities will I remember no more.

Hebrews 8:12

I, even I, am he that blotteth out thy transgressions for mine own sake, and will not remember thy sins.

Isaiah 43:25

Let the wicked forsake his way, and the unrighteous man his thoughts: and let him return unto the Lord, and he will have mercy upon him; and to our God, for he will abundantly pardon.

Isaiah 55:7

I acknowledged my sin unto thee, and mine iniquity have I not hid. I said, I will confess my transgressions unto the Lord; and thou forgavest the iniquity of my sin. Selah.

Psalm 32:5

If we confess our sins, he is faithful and just to forgive us our sins, and to cleanse us from all unrighteousness.

I John 1:9

Blessed is he whose trangression is forgiven, whose sin is covered.

Psalm 32:1

And I heard a loud voice saying in heaven, Now is come salvation, and strength, and the kingdom of our God, and the power of his Christ: for the accuser of our brethren is cast down, which accused them before our God day and night.

Revelation 12:10, 11

When Jesus had lifted up himself, and saw none but the woman, he said unto her, Woman, where are those thine accusers? hath no man condemned thee?

She said, No man, Lord. And Jesus said unto her, Neither do I condemn thee: go, and sin no more.

John 8:10, 11

And they shall teach no more every man his neighbour, and every man his brother, saying, Know the Lord: for they shall all know me, from the least of them unto the greatest of them, saith the Lord: for I will forgive their iniquity, and I will remember their sin no more.

Jeremiah 31:34

Let us draw near with a true heart in full assurance of faith, having our hearts sprinkled from an evil conscience, and our bodies washed with pure water.

Hebrews 10:22

For if ye turn again unto the Lord, your brethren and your children shall find compassion before them that lead them captive, so that they shall come again into this land: for the Lord your God is gracious and merciful, and will not turn away his face from you, if ye return unto him.

II Chronicles 30:9

Confused

For God is not the author of confusion, but of peace, as in all churches of the saints.

I Corinthians 14:33

For God hath not given us the spirit of fear; but of power, and of love, and of a sound mind.

II Timothy 1:7

For where envying and strife is, there is confusion and every evil work.

But the wisdom that is from above is first pure, then peaceable, gentle, and easy to be entreated, full of mercy and good fruits, without partiality, and without hypocrisy.

And the fruit of righteousness is sown in peace of them that make peace.

James 3:16-18

For the Lord God will help me; therefore shall I not be confounded: therefore have I set my face like a flint, and I know that I shall not be ashamed.

Isaiah 50:7

Beloved, think it not strange concerning the fiery trial which is to try you, as though some strange thing happened unto you: But rejoice, inasmuch as ye are partakers of Christ's sufferings; that, when his glory shall be revealed, ye may be glad also with exceeding joy.

I Peter 4:12, 13

If any of you lack wisdom, let him ask of God, that giveth to all men liberally, and upbraideth not; and it shall be given him.

James 1:5

Trust in the Lord with all thine heart; and lean not unto thine own understanding.

In all thy ways acknowledge him, and he shall direct thy paths.

Proverbs 3:5, 6

I will instruct thee and teach thee in the way which thou shalt go: I will guide thee with mine eye.

Psalm 32:8

Great peace have they which love thy law: and nothing shall offend them.

Psalm 119:165

Cast thy burden upon the Lord, and he shall sustain thee: he shall never suffer the righteous to be moved.

Psalm 55:22

When thou passest through the waters, I will be with thee; and through the rivers, they shall not overflow thee: when thou walkest through the fire, thou shalt not be burned; neither shall the flame kindle upon thee.

Isaiah 43:2

He giveth power to the faint; and to them that have no might he increaseth strength.

Isaiah 40:29

And thine ears shall hear a word behind thee, saying, This is the way, walk ye in it, when ye turn to the right hand, and when ye turn to the left.

Isaiah 30:21

Be careful for nothing; but in every thing by prayer and supplication with thanksgiving let your requests be made known unto God.

And the peace of God, which passeth all understanding, shall keep your hearts and minds through Christ Jesus.

Philippians 4:6, 7

Tempted

Wherefore let him that thinketh he standeth take heed lest he fall.

There hath no temptation taken you but such as is common to man: but God is faithful, who will not suffer you to be tempted above that ye are able; but will with the temptation also make a way of escape, that ye may be able to bear it.

I Corinthians 10:12, 13

Seeing then that we have a great high priest, that is passed into the heavens, Jesus the Son of God, let us hold fast our profession.

For we have not an high priest which cannot be touched with the feeling of our infirmities; but was in all points tempted like as we are, yet without sin.

Let us therefore come boldly unto the throne of grace, that we may obtain mercy, and find grace to help in time of need.

Hebrews 4:14-16

For in that he himself hath suffered being tempted, he is able to succour them that are tempted.

Hebrews 2:18

The Lord knoweth how to deliver the godly out of temptations,

II Peter 2:9a

For sin shall not have dominion over you: for ye are not under the law, but under grace.

Romans 6:14

Thy word have I hid in mine heart, that I might not sin against thee.

Psalm 119:11

Let no man say when he is tempted, I am tempted of God: for God cannot be tempted with evil, neither tempteth he any man:

But every man is tempted, when he is drawn away of his own lust, and enticed.

James 1:13, 14

He that covereth his sins shall not prosper: but whoso confesseth and forsaketh them shall have mercy.

Proverbs 28:13

If we confess our sins, he is faithful and just to forgive us our sins, and to cleanse us from all unrighteousness.

I John 1:9

Be sober, be vigilant; because your adversary the devil, as a roaring lion, walketh about, seeking whom he may devour:

Whom resist stedfast in the faith, knowing that the same afflictions are accomplished in your brethren that are in the world.

I Peter 5:8, 9

Finally, my brethren, be strong in the Lord, and in the power of his might.

Put on the whole armour of God, that ye may be able to stand against the wiles of the devil.

Above all, taking the shield of faith, wherewith ye shall be able to quench all the fiery darts of the wicked.

Ephesians 6:10, 11, 16

Submit yourselves therefore to God. Resist the devil, and he will flee from you.

James 4:7

Ye are of God, little children, and have overcome them: because greater is he that is in you, than he that is in the world.

I John 4:4

My brethren, count it all joy when ye fall into divers temptations;

Knowing this, that the trying of your faith worketh patience.

Blessed is the man that endureth temptation: for when he is tried, he shall receive the crown of life, which the Lord hath promised to them that love him.

James 1:2, 3, 12

Now unto him that is able to keep you from falling, and to present you faultless before the presence of this glory with exceeding joy.

To the only wise God our Saviour, be glory and majesty.

Jude 24, 25a

Wherein ye greatly rejoice, though now for a season, if need be, ye are in heaviness through manifold temptations:

That the trial of your faith, being much more precious than of gold that perisheth, though it be tried with fire, might be found unto praise and honour and glory and the appearing of Jesus Christ:

I Peter 1:6, 7

Angry

Wherefore, my beloved brethren, let every man be swift to hear, slow to speak, slow to wrath:

For the wrath of man worketh not the righteousness of God.

James 1:19, 20

Be ye angry, and sin not: let not the sun go down upon your wrath:

Ephesians 4:26

A soft answer turneth away wrath: but grievous words stir up anger.

Proverbs 15:1

For if ye forgive men their trespasses, your heavenly Father will also forgive you:

Matthew 6:14

He that is slow to wrath is of great understanding: but he that is hasty of spirit exalteth folly.

Proverbs 14:29

He that is slow to anger is better than the mighty; and he that ruleth his spirit than he that taketh a city.

Proverbs 16:32

Be not hasty in thy spirit to be angry: for anger resteth in the bosom of fools.

Ecclesiastes 7:9

Dearly beloved, avenge not yourselves, but rather give place unto wrath: for it is written, Vengeance is mine; I will repay, saith the Lord.

Romans 12:19

If thine enemy be hungry, give him bread to eat; and if he be thirsty, give him water to drink:

For thou shalt heap coals of fire upon his head, and the Lord shall reward thee.

Proverbs 25:21, 22

For we know him that hath said, Vengeance belongeth unto me, I will recompense, saith the Lord. And again, The Lord shall judge his people.

Hebrews 10:30

Let all bitterness, and wrath, and anger, and clamour, and evil speaking, be put away from you, with all malice:

And be ye kind one to another, tenderhearted, forgiving one another, even as God for Christ's sake hath forgiven you.

Ephesians 4:31, 32

But I say unto you, That whosoever is angry with his brother without a cause shall be in danger of the judgment: and whosoever shall say to his brother, Ra'-ca, shall be in danger of the council: but whosoever shall say, Thou fool, shall be in danger of hell fire.

Therefore if thou bring thy gift to the altar, and there rememberest that thy brother hath ought against thee;

Leave there thy gift before the alter, and go thy way; first be reconciled to thy brother, and then come and offer thy gift.

Matthew 5:22-24

A wise man feareth, and departeth from evil: but the fool rageth, and is confident.

He that is soon angry dealeth foolishly: and a man of wicked devices is hated.

Proverbs 14:16, 17

But now ye also put off all these; anger, wrath, malice, blasphemy, filthy communication out of your mouth

Colossians 3:8

Cease from anger, and forsake wrath: fret not thyself in any wise to do evil.

Psalm 37:8

Rebellious

Obey them that have the rule over you, and submit yourselves: for they watch for your souls, as they that must give account, that they may do it with joy, and not with grief: for that is unprofitable for you.

Hebrews 13:17

A wise man feareth, and departeth from evil: But the fool rageth, and is confident.

He that is soon angry dealeth foolishly: and a man of wicked devices is hated.

Proverbs 14:16, 17

And Samuel said, Hath the Lord as great delight in burnt offerings and sacrifices, as in obeying the voice of the Lord? Behold, to obey is better than sacrifice, and to hearken than the fat of rams.

For rebellion is as the sin of witchcraft, and stubborness is as iniquity and idolatry. Because thou hast rejected the word of the Lord, he hath also rejected thee from being king.

I Samuel 15:22, 23

Wherefore gird up the loins of your mind, be sober, and hope to the end for the grace that is to be brought unto you at the revelation of Jesus Christ;

As obedient children, not fashioning yourselves according to the former lusts in your ignorance:

I Peter 1:13, 14

If ye be willing and obedient, ye shall eat the good of the land:

But if ye refuse and rebel, ye shall be devoured with the sword: for the mouth of the Lord hath spoken it.

Isaiah 1:19, 20

Submit yourselves to every ordinance of man for the Lord's sake: whether it be to the king, as supreme;

Or unto governors, as unto them that are sent by him for the punishment of evil-doers, and for the praise of them that do well.

For so is the will of God, that with well-doing ye may put to silence the ignorance of foolish men:

I Peter 2:13-15

Let this mind be in you, which was also in Christ Jesus:

Who, being in the form of God, thought it not robbery to be equal with God:

But made himself of no reputation, and took upon him the form of a servant, and was made in the likeness of men:

And being found in fashion as a man, he humbled himself, and became obedient unto death, even the death of the cross.

Philippians 2:5-8

Though he were a Son, yet learned he obedience by the things which he suffered;

Hebrews 5:8

Likewise, ye younger, submit yourselves unto the elder. Yea, all of you be subject one to another, and be clothed with humility: for God resisteth the proud, and giveth grace to the humble.

Humble yourselves therefore under the mighty hand of God, that he may exalt you in due time:

I Peter 5:5, 6

Submitting yourselves one to another in the fear of God.

Ephesians 5:21

There shall no evil happen to the just: but the wicked shall be filled with mischief.

Proverbs 12:21

Let not sin therefore reign in your mortal body, that ye should obey it in the lusts thereof.

Neither yield ye your members as instruments of unrighteousness unto sin: but yield yourselves unto God, as those that are alive from the dead, and your members as instruments of righteousness unto God.

Romans 6:12, 13

This I say therefore, and testify in the Lord, that ye henceforth walk not as other Gentiles walk, in the vanity of their mind,

Having the understanding darkened, being alienated from the life of God through the ignorance that is in them, because of the blindness of their heart:

Ephesians 4:17, 18

For ye were sometimes darkness, but now are ye light in the Lord: walk as children of light:

Ephesians 5:8

Submit yourselves therefore to God. Resist the devil, and he will flee from you.

James 4:7

What To Do When You Are . . .

WHAT TO DO WHEN YOU ARE
Experiencing Fear

For God hath not given us the spirit of fear; but of power, and of love, and of a sound mind.

II Timothy 1:7

For ye have not received the spirit of bondage again to fear; but ye have received the Spirit of adoption, whereby we cry, Abba, Father.

Romans 8:15

There is no fear in love; but perfect love casteth out fear: because fear hath torment. He that feareth is not made perfect in love.

I John 4:18

He that dwelleth in the secret place of the most High shall abide under the shadow of the Almighty.

Psalm 91:1

He shall cover thee with his feathers, and under his wings shalt thou trust: his trust shall be thy shield and buckler.

Thou shalt not be afraid for the terror by night; nor for the arrow that flieth by day;

Nor for the pestilence that walketh in darkness; nor for the destruction that wasteth at noonday.

A thousand shall fall at thy side, and ten thousand at thy right hand; but it shall not come nigh thee.

Psalm 91:4-7

There shall no evil befall thee, neither shall any plague come nigh thy dwelling.

For he shall give his angels charge over thee, to keep thee in all thy ways.

Psalm 91:10, 11

Be not afraid of sudden fear, neither of the desolation of the wicked, when it cometh. For the Lord shall be thy confidence, and shall keep thy foot from being taken.

Proverbs 3:25, 26

In righteousness shalt thou be established: thou shalt be far from oppression; for thou shalt not fear: and from terror; for it shall not come near thee.

Isaiah 54:14

In God have I put my trust: I will not be afraid what man can do unto me.

Psalm 56:11

Yea, though I walk through the valley of the shadow of death, I will fear no evil: for thou art with me; thy rod and thy staff they comfort me.

Thou preparest a table before me in the presence of mine enemies: thou anointest my head with oil; my cup runneth over.

Psalm 23:4, 5

For whom he did foreknow, he also did predestinate to be conformed to the image of his Son, that he might be the firstborn among many brethren.

What shall we then say to these things? If God be for us, who can be against us?

Who shall separate us from the love of Christ? shall tribulation, or distress, or persecution, or famine, or nakedness, or peril, or sword?

As it is written, For thy sake we are killed all the day long; we are accounted as sheep for the slaughter.

Nay, in all these things we are more than conquerors through him that loved us.

For I am persuaded, that neither death, nor life, nor angels, nor principalities, nor powers, nor things present, nor things to come,

Nor height, nor depth, nor any other creature, shall be able to separate us from the love of God, which is in Christ Jesus our Lord.

Romans 8:29, 31, 35-39

Be of good courage, and he shall strengthen your heart, all ye that hope in the Lord.

Psalm 31:24

Peace I leave with you, my peace I give unto you: not as the world giveth, give I unto you. Let not your heart be troubled, neither let it be afraid.

John 14:27

The Lord is my light and my salvation; whom shall I fear? the Lord is the strength of my life; of whom shall I be afraid?

Though an host should encamp against me, my heart shall not fear; though war should rise against me, in this will I be confident.

Psalm 27:1, 3

So that we may boldly say, The Lord is my helper, and I will not fear what man shall do unto me.

Hebrews 13:6

WHAT TO DO WHEN YOU ARE
Mentally Disturbed

For God hath not given us the spirit of fear; but of power, and of love, and of a sound mind.

II Timothy 1:7

Fear thou not; for I am with thee: be not dismayed; for I am thy God: I will strengthen thee; yea, I will help thee; yea, I will uphold thee with the right hand of my righteousness.

Isaiah 41:10

For God is not the author of confusion, but of peace,

I Corinthians 14:33a

For where envying and strife is, there is confusion and every evil work:

But the wisdom that is from above is first pure, then peaceable, gentle, and easy to be intreated, full of mercy and good fruits, without partiality, and without hypocrisy.

And the fruit of righteousness is sown in peace of them that make peace.

James 3:16-18

Wherefore also it is contained in the scripture, Behold, I lay in Sion a chief cornerstone, elect, precious: and he that believeth on him shall not be confounded.

I Peter 2:6

For the Lord God will help me; therefore shall I not be confounded: therefore have I set my face like a flint, and I know that I shall not be ashamed.

Isaiah 50:7

Cast thy burden upon the Lord, and he shall sustain thee: he shall never suffer the righteous to be moved.

Psalm 55:22

Be careful for nothing; but in every thing by prayer and supplication with thanksgiving let your requests be made known unto God.

And the peace of God, which passeth all understanding, shall keep your hearts and minds through Christ Jesus.

Philippians 4:6, 7

Great peace have they which love thy law: and nothing shall offend them.

Psalm 119:165

For his anger endureth but a moment; in his favour is life: weeping may endure for a night, but joy cometh in the morning.

Psalm 30:5

When thou passest through the waters, I will be with thee; and through the rivers, they shall not overflow thee: when thou walkest through the fire, thou shalt not be burned; neither shall the flame kindle upon thee.

Isaiah 43:2

He healeth the broken in heart, and bindeth up their wounds.

Psalm 147:3

Blessed be God, even the Father of our Lord Jesus Christ, the Father of mercies, and the God of all comfort.

Who comforteth us in all our tribulation, that we may be able to comfort them which are in any trouble, by the comfort wherewith we ourselves are comforted of God.

II Corinthians 1:3, 4

Finally, brethren, whatsoever things are true, whatsoever things are honest, whatsoever things are just, whatsoever things are pure, whatsoever things are lovely, whatsoever things are of good report; if there be any virtue, and if there be any praise, think on these things.

Philippians 4:8

For I am persuaded, that neither death, nor life, nor angels, nor principalities, nor powers, nor things present, nor things to come,

Nor height, nor depth, nor any other creature, shall be able to separate us from the love of God which is in Christ Jesus our Lord.

Romans 8:38, 39

WHAT TO DO WHEN YOU ARE

In Need Of Courage

Wait on the Lord: be of good courage, and he shall strengthen thine heart: wait, I say, on the Lord.

Psalm 27:14

For his anger endureth but a moment; in his favour is life: weeping may endure for a night, but joy cometh in the morning.

Psalm 30:5

When thou passest through the waters, I will be with thee; and through the rivers, they shall not overflow thee: when thou walkest through the fire, thou shalt not be burned; neither shall the flame kindle upon thee.

Isaiah 43:2

Beloved, think it not strange concerning the fiery trial which is to try you, as though some strange thing happened unto you:

But rejoice, inasmuch as ye are partakers of Christ's sufferings; that when his glory shall be revealed, ye may be glad also with exceeding joy.

I Peter 4:12, 13

For I am persuaded, that neither death, nor life, nor angels, nor principalities, nor powers, nor things present, nor things to come,

Nor height, nor depth, nor any other creature, shall be able to separate us from the love of God which is in Christ Jesus our Lord.

Romans 8:38, 39

Fear thou not: for I am with thee: be not dismayed; for I am thy God: I will strengthen thee; yea, I will help thee; yea, I will uphold thee with the right hand of my righteousness.

Isaiah 41:10

The eternal God is thy refuge, and underneath are the everlasting arms: and he shall thrust out the enemy from before thee; and shall say, Destroy them.

Deuteronomy 33:27

I shall not die, but live, and declare the works of the Lord.

Psalm 118:17

I can do all things through Christ which strengtheneth me.

Philippians 4:13

Be of good courage, and he shall strengthen your heart, all ye that hope in the Lord.

Psalm 31:24

But they that wait upon the Lord shall renew their strength; they shall mount up with wings as eagles; they shall run and not be weary; and they shall walk and not faint.

Isaiah 40:31

Be careful for nothing; but in every thing by prayer and supplication with thanksgiving let your requests be made known unto God.

Philippians 4:6

Finally, brethren, whatsoever things are true, whatsoever things are honest, whatsoever things are just, whatsoever things are pure, whatsoever things are lovely, whatsoever things are of good report; if there be any virtue, and if there be any praise, think on these things.

Philippians 4:8

Therefore the redeemed of the Lord shall return, and come with singing unto Zion; and everlasting joy shall be upon their head: they shall obtain gladness and joy; and sorrow and mourning shall flee away.

Isaiah 51:11

In Need Of Patience

But the fruit of the Spirit is love, joy, peace, longsuffering, gentleness, goodness, faith.

Galatians 5:22

But they that wait upon the Lord shall renew their strength; they shall mount up with wings as eagles; they shall run, and not be weary; and they shall walk, and not faint.

Isaiah 40:31

Wait on the Lord: be of good courage, and he shall strengthen thine heart: wait, I say, on the Lord.

Psalm 27:14

It is good that a man should both hope and quietly wait for the salvation of the Lord.

Lamentations 3:26

But if we hope for that we see not, then do we with patience wait for it.

Romans 8:25

Rest in the Lord, and wait patiently for him: fret not thyself because of him who prospereth in his way, because of the man who bringeth wicked devices to pass.

Psalms 37:7

That ye be not slothful, but followers of them who through faith land patience inherit the promises.

Hebrews 6:12

Cast not away therefore your confidence, which hath great recompence of reward.

For ye have need of patience, that, after ye have done the will of God, ye might receive the promise.

For yet a little while, and he that shall come will come, and will not tarry.

Hebrews 10:35-37

Wherefore seeing we also are compassed about with so great a cloud of witnesses, let us lay aside every weight, and the sin which doth so easily beset us, and let us run with patience the race that is set before us,

Hebrews 12:1

Better is the end of a thing than the beginning thereof: and the patient in spirit is better than the proud in spirit.

Be not hasty in thy spirit to be angry: for anger resteth in the bosom of fools.

Ecclesiastes 7:8, 9

For whatsoever things were written aforetime were written for our learning, that we through patience and comfort of the scriptures might have hope.

Now the God of patience and consolation grant you to be likeminded one toward another according to Christ Jesus.

Romans 15:4, 5

Cease from anger, and forsake wrath: fret not thyself in any wise to do evil.

For evildoers shall be cut off: but those that wait upon the Lord, they shall inherit the earth.

Psalm 37:8, 9

I waited patiently for the Lord; and he inclined unto me, and heard my cry.

Psalm 40:1

And not only so, but we glory in tribulations also: knowing that tribulation worketh patience;

And patience, experience; and experience, hope:

And hope maketh not ashamed; because the love of God is shed abroad in our hearts by the Holy Ghost which is given unto us.

Romans 5:3-5

Knowing this, that the trying of your faith worketh patience.

But let patience have her perfect work, that ye may be perfect and entire, wanting nothing.

James 1:3, 4

Be patient therefore, brethren, unto the coming of the Lord. Behold, the husbandman waiteth for the precious fruit of the earth, and hath long patience for it, until he receive the early and latter rain.

Be ye also patient; stablish your hearts: for the coming of the Lord draweth nigh.

James 5:7, 8

WHAT TO DO WHEN YOU ARE
In Need Of Peace

Thou wilt keep him in perfect peace, whose mind is stayed on thee: because he trusteth in thee.

Isaiah 26:3

Peace, I leave with you, my peace I give unto you; not as the world giveth, give I unto you. Let not your heart be troubled, neither let it be afraid.

John 14:27

Be careful for nothing; but in every thing by prayer and supplication with thanksgiving let your requests be made known unto God.

And the peace of God, which passeth all understanding, shall keep your hearts and minds through Christ Jesus.

Philippians 4:6, 7

Therefore being justified by faith, we have peace with God through our Lord Jesus Christ:

Romans 5:1

Lord thou wilt ordain peace for us: for thou also hast wrought all our works in us.

Isaiah 26:12

For ye shall go out with joy, and be led forth with peace: the mountains and the hills shall break forth before you into singing, and all the trees of the field shall clap their hands.

Isaiah 55:12

Mark the perfect man, and behold the upright: for the end of that man is peace.

Psalm 37:37

For to be carnally minded is death: but to be spiritually minded is life and peace.

Romans 8:6

Great peace have they which love thy law: and nothing shall offend them.

Psalm 119:165

He shall enter into peace: they shall rest in their beds, each one walking in his uprightness.

Isaiah 57:2

For the kingdom of God is not meat and drink; but righteousness, and peace, and joy in the Holy Ghost.

For he that in these things serveth Christ is acceptable to God, and approved of men.

Let us therefore follow after the things which make for peace, and things wherewith one may edify another.

Romans 14:17-19

But the meek shall inherit the earth; and shall delight themselves in the abundance of peace.

Psalm 37:11

Finally, brethren, farewell. Be perfect, be of good comfort, be of one mind, live in peace; and the God of love and peace shall be with you.

II Corinthians 13:11

Now the God of hope fill you with all joy and peace in believing, that ye may abound in hope, through the power of the Holy Ghost.

Romans 15:13

Lukewarm Spiritually

Be watchful, and strengthen the things which remain, that are ready to die: for I have not found thy works perfect before God.

I know thy works, that thou are neither cold nor hot: I would thou wert cold or hot.

So then because thou are lukewarm, and neither cold nor hot, I will spue thee out of my mouth.

Revelation 3:2, 15, 16

Nevertheless I have somewhat against thee, because thou hast left thy first love.

Revelation 2:4

O Ephraim, what shall I do unto thee? O Judah, what shall I do unto thee? for your goodness is as a morning cloud, and as the early dew it goeth away.

Hosea 6:4

Only take heed to thyself, and keep thy soul diligently, lest thou forget the things which thine eyes have seen, and lest they depart from thy heart all the days of thy life: but teach them thy sons, and thy sons' sons;

Deuteronomy 4:9

Beware that thou forget not the Lord thy God, in not keeping his commandments, and his judgments, and his statutes, which I command thee this day.

Lest when thou hast eaten and art full, and hast built goodly houses, and dwelt therein;

And when thy herds and thy flocks multiply, and thy silver and thy gold is multiplied, and all that thou hast is multiplied;

Then thine heart be lifted up, and thou forget the Lord thy God, which brought thee forth out of the land of Egypt, from the house of bondage;

Deuteronomy 8:11-14

If we have forgotten the name of our God, or stretched out our hands to a strange god;

Shall not God search this out? for he knoweth the secrets of the heart.

Psalm 44:20, 21

Take heed, brethren, lest there be in any of you an evil heart of unbelief, in departing from the living God.

But exhort one another daily, while it is called Today; lest any of you be hardened through the deceitfulness of sin.

Hebrews 3:12, 13

Of whom we have many things to say, and hard to be uttered, seeing ye are dull of hearing.

For when for the time ye ought to be teachers, ye have need that one teach you again which be the first principles of the oracles of God; and are become such as have need of milk, and not of strong meat.

Hebrews 5:11, 12

Looking diligently lest any man fail of the grace of God; lest any root of bitterness springing up trouble you, and thereby many be defiled;

Hebrews 12:15

For if after they have escaped the pollutions of the world through the knowledge of the Lord and Saviour Jesus Christ, they are again entangled therein, and overcome, the latter end is worse with them than the beginning.

For it had been better for them not to have known the way of righteousness, than, after they have known it, to turn from the holy commandment delivered unto them.

II Peter 2:20, 21

Thus saith the Lord, Stand ye in the ways, and see, and ask for the old paths, where is the good way, and walk therein, and ye shall find rest for your souls. But they said, We will not walk therein.

Jeremiah 6:16

If we confess our sins, he is faithful and just to forgive us our sins, and to cleanse us from all unrighteousness.

I John 1:9

Even from the days of your fathers ye are gone away from mine ordinances, and have not kept them. Return unto me, and I will return unto you, saith the Lord of hosts.

Malachi 3:7a

WHAT TO DO WHEN YOU ARE

In Grief

But I would not have you to be ignorant, brethren, concerning them which
are asleep, that ye sorrow not, even as others
which have no hope.

For if we believe that Jesus died and
rose again, even so them also which sleep in
Jesus will God bring with him.

I Thessalonians 4:13, 14

For the Lord hath comforted his people, and will have mercy upon his afflicted.

Isaiah 49:13b

When thou passest through the waters,
I will be with thee; and through the rivers,
they shall not overflow thee: when thou
walkest through the fire, thou shalt not be
burned; neither shall the flame kindle upon
thee.

Isaiah 43:2

Now our Lord Jesus Christ himself,
and God, even our Father, which hath loved
us, and hath given us everlasting consolation
and good hope through grace,

Comfort your hearts, and stablish you
in every good word and work.

II Thessalonians 2:16, 17

Blessed are they that mourn: for they shall be comforted.

Matthew 5:4

Blessed be God, even the Father of our Lord Jesus Christ, the Father of mercies, and the God of all comfort;

Who comforteth us in all our tribulation, that we may be able to comfort them which are in any trouble, by the comfort wherewith we ourselves are comforted of God.

II Corinthians 1:3, 4

The Spirit of the Lord God is upon me; because the Lord hath anointed me to preach good tidings unto the meek; he hath sent me to bind up the broken-hearted, to proclaim liberty to the captives, and the opening of the prison to them that are bound;

To Proclaim the acceptable year of the Lord, and the day of vengeance of our God; to comfort all that mourn;

To appoint unto them that mourn in Zion, to give unto them beauty for ashes, the oil of joy for mourning, the garment of praise for the spirit of heaviness; that they might be called trees of righteousness, the planting of the Lord, that he might be glorified.

Isaiah 61:1-3

This is my comfort in my affliction: for thy word hath quickened me.

Psalm 119:50

Casting all your care upon him; for he careth for you.

I Peter 5:7

O death, where is thy sting? O grave, where is thy victory?

The sting of death is sin; and the strength of sin is the law.

But thanks be to God, which giveth us the victory through our Lord Jesus Christ.

I Corinthians 15:55-57

Yea, though I walk through the valley of the shadow of death, I will fear no evil: for thou art with me; thy rod and thy staff they comfort me.

Psalm 23:4

For we have not an high priest which cannot be touched with the feeling of our infirmities; but was in all points tempted like as we are, yet without sin.

Let us therefore come boldly unto the throne of grace, that we may obtain mercy, and find grace to help in time of need.

Hebrews 4:15, 16

Fear thou not; for I am with thee: be not dismayed; for I am thy God: I will strengthen thee; yea, I will help thee; yea, I will uphold thee with the right hand of my righteousness.

Isaiah 41:10

Therefore the redeemed of the Lord shall return, and come with singing unto Zion; and everlasting joy shall be upon their head: they shall obtain gladness and joy; and sorrow and mourning shall flee away.

Isaiah 51:11

We are confident, I say, and willing rather to be absent from the body, and to be present with the Lord.

II Corinthians 5:8

And God shall wipe away all tears from their eyes; and there shall be no more death, neither sorrow, nor crying, neither shall there be any more pain: for the former things are passed away.

Revelation 21:4

In Doubt About God

And Jesus answering saith unto them,
Have faith in God.

For verily I say unto you, That whosoever shall say unto this mountain, Be thou
removed, and be thou cast into the sea; and
shall not doubt in his heart, but shall believe
that those things which he saith shall come to
pass: he shall have whatsoever he saith.

Therefore I say unto you, What things
soever ye desire, when you pray, believe that
ye receive them, and ye shall have them.

Mark 11:22-24

And seek not ye what ye shall eat, or
what ye shall drink, neither be ye of doubtful
mind.

For all these things do the nations of
the world seek after: and your Father
knoweth that ye have need of these things.

But rather seek ye the kingdom of God;
and all these things shall be added unto you.

Luke 12:29-31

He staggered not at the promise of God
through unbelief; but was strong in faith,
giving glory to God;

And being fully persuaded that, what he had promised, he was able also to perform.

Romans 4:20, 21

My counsel shall stand, and I will do all my pleasure:

I have spoken it, I will also bring it to pass; I have purposed it, I will also do it.

Isaiah 46:10b, 11b

Faithful is he that calleth you, who also will do it.

I Thessalonians 5:24

The Lord is not slack concerning his promise, as some men count slackness; but is longsuffering to us-ward, not willing that any should perish, but that all should come to repentance.

II Peter 3:9

As for God, his way is perfect: the word of the Lord is tried: he is a buckler to all those that trust in him.

Psalm 18:30

Behold, the Lord's hand is not shortened, that it cannot save; neither his ear heavy, that it cannot hear:

Isaiah 59:1

Beloved, think it not strange concerning the fiery trial which is to try you, as though some strange thing happened unto you:

But rejoice, inasmuch as you are partakers of Christ's sufferings; that, when his glory shall be revealed, ye may be glad also with exceeding joy.

I Peter 4:12, 13

So then faith cometh by hearing, and hearing by the word of God.

Romans 10:17

For as the rain cometh down, and the snow from heaven, and returneth not thither, but watereth the earth, and maketh it bring forth and bud, that it may give seed to the sower, and bread to the eater:

So shall my word be that goeth forth out of my mouth: it shall not return unto me void, but it shall accomplish that which I please, and it shall prosper in the thing whereto I sent it.

Isaiah 55:10, 11

What To Do When . . .

You Need Confidence

I can do all things through Christ which strengtheneth me.

Philippians 4:13

So that we may boldly say, The Lord is my helper, and I will not fear what man shall do unto me.

Hebrews 13:6

Cast not away therefore your confidence, which hath great recompence of reward.

For ye have need of patience, that, after ye have done the will of God, ye might receive the promise.

Hebrews 10:35, 36

Being confident of this very thing, that he which hath begun a good work in you will perform it until the day of Jesus Christ:

Philippians 1:6

The Lord God is my strength, and he will make my feet like hinds' feet, and he will make me to walk upon mine high places. To the chief singer on my stringed instruments.

Habakkuk 3:19

Nay, in all these things we are more than conquerors through him that loved us.

Romans 8:37

And this is the confidence that we have in him, that, if we ask any thing according to his will, he heareth us:

And if we know that he hear us, whatsoever we ask, we know that we have the petitions that we desired of him.

I John 5:14, 15

Verily, verily, I say unto you, He that believeth on me, the works that I do shall he do also; and greater works than these shall he do; because I go unto my Father.

John 14:12

Then he answered and spake unto me, saying, This is the word of the Lord unto Zerubbabel, saying, Not by might, nor by power, but by my spirit, saith the Lord of hosts.

Zechariah 4:6

When thou passest through the waters, I will be with thee; and through the rivers, they shall not overflow thee: when thou walkest through the fire, thou shalt not be burned; neither shall the flame kindle upon thee.

Isaiah 43:2

For the Lord shall be thy confidence, and shall keep thy foot from being taken.

Proverbs 3:26

I rejoice therefore that I have confidence in you in all things.

II Corinthians 7:16

In whom we have boldness and access with confidence by the faith of him.

Ephesians 3:12

Beloved, if our heart condemn us not, then have we confidence toward God.

I John 3:21

But they that wait upon the Lord shall renew their strength; they shall mount up with wings as eagles; they shall run, and not be weary; and they shall walk, and not faint.

Isaiah 40:31

WHAT TO DO WHEN
Troubles Hit Your Life:

The Lord is good, a strong hold in the day of trouble; and he knoweth them that trust in him.

Nahum 1:7

We are troubled on every side, yet not distressed; we are perplexed, but not in despair;

Persecuted, but not forsaken; cast down, but not destroyed;

II Corinthians 4:8, 9

Though I walk in the midst of trouble, thou wilt revive me: thou shalt stretch forth thine hand against the wrath of mine enemies, and thy right hand shall save me.

Psalm 138:7

Let not your heart be troubled: ye believe in God, believe also in me.

John 14:1

When thou passest through the waters, I will be with thee: and through the rivers, they shall not overflow thee: when thou walkest through the fire, thou shalt not be burned; neither shall the flame kindle upon thee.

Isaiah 43:2

And we know that all things work together for good to them that love God, to them who are the called according to His purpose.

Romans 8:28

I will be glad and rejoice in thy mercy: for thou hast considered my trouble; thou hast known my soul in adversities;

Psalm 31:7

I will lift up mine eyes unto the hills, from whence cometh my help. My help cometh from the Lord, which made heaven and earth.

Psalm 121:1, 2

For we have not an high priest which cannot be touched with the feeling of our infirmities; but was in all points tempted like as we are, yet without sin.

Let us therefore come boldly unto the throne of grace, that we may obtain mercy, and find grace to help in time of need.

Hebrews 4:15, 16

Casting all your care upon him; for he careth for you.

I Peter 5:7

Take therefore no thought for the morrow: for the morrow shall take thought for the things of itself. Sufficient unto the day is the evil thereof.

Matthew 6:34

Blessed be God, even the Father of our Lord Jesus Christ, the Father of mercies, and the God of all comfort;

Who comforteth us in all our tribulation, that we may be able to comfort them which are in any trouble, by the comfort wherewith we ourselves are comforted of God.

II Corinthians 1:3, 4

Be careful for nothing; but in every thing by prayer and supplication with thanksgiving let your requests be made known unto God.

And the peace of God, which passeth all understanding, shall keep your hearts and minds through Christ Jesus.

Philippians 4:6, 7

Therefore the redeemed of the Lord shall return, and come with singing unto Zion; and everlasting joy shall be upon their head: they shall obtain gladness and joy; and sorrow and mourning shall flee away.

Isaiah 51:11

You Have A Physical Sickness

Beloved, I wish above all things that thou mayest prosper and be in health, even as thy soul prospereth.

III John 2

And Jesus went about all the cities and villages, teaching in their synagogues, and preaching the gospel of the kingdom, and healing every sickness and every disease among the people.

Matthew 9:35

And the whole multitude sought to touch him: for there went virtue out of him, and healed them all.

Luke 6:19

Jesus Christ the same yesterday, and to-day, and for ever.

Hebrews 13:8

Who his own self bare our sins in his own body on the tree, that we, being dead to sins, should live unto righteousness: by whose stripes ye were healed.

I Peter 2:24

Who forgiveth all thine iniquites; who healeth all thy diseases;

Psalm 103:3

But he was wounded for our transgressions, he was bruised for our iniquities: the chastisement of our peace was upon him; and with his stripes we are healed.

Isaiah 53:5

Heal me, O Lord, and I shall be healed; save me, and I shall be saved: for thou art my praise.

Jeremiah 17:14

For I will restore health unto thee, and I will heal thee of thy wounds, saith the Lord;

Jeremiah 30:17a

And said, If thou wilt diligently hearken to the voice of the Lord thy God, and wilt do that which is right in his sight, and wilt give ear to his commandments, and keep all his statutes, I will put none of these diseases upon thee, which I have brought upon the Egyptians: for I am the Lord that healeth thee.

Exodus 15:26

My son, attend to my words; incline thine ear unto my sayings.

Let them not depart from thine eyes; keep them in the midst of thine heart.

For they are life unto those that find them, and health to all their flesh.

Proverbs 4:20-22

He sent his word, and healed them, and delivered them from their destructions.

Psalm 107:20

The centurion answered and said, Lord, I am not worthy that thou shouldest come under my roof: but speak the word only, and my servant shall be healed.

Matthew 8:8

Is any sick among you? let him call for the elders of the church; and let them pray over him, anointing him with oil in the name of the Lord:

And the prayer of faith shall save the sick, and the Lord shall raise him up; and if he have committed sins, they shall be forgiven him.

James 5:14, 15

And these signs shall follow them that believe; In my name shall they cast out devils; they shall speak with new tongues;

They shall take up serpents; and if they drink any deadly thing, it shall not hurt them; they shall lay hands on the sick, and they shall recover.

Mark 16:17, 18

When You Are In Financial Trouble

Beloved, I wish above all things that thou mayest prosper and be in health, even as thy soul prospereth.

III John 2

I have been young, and now am old; yet have I not seen the righteous forsaken, nor his seed begging bread.

Psalm 37:25

The young lions do lack, and suffer hunger: but they that seek the Lord shall not want any good thing.

Psalm 34:10

The Lord is my shepherd; I shall not want.

Psalm 23:1

And all these blessings shall come on thee, and overtake thee, if thou shalt hearken unto the voice of the Lord thy God.

Blessed shalt thou be in the city, and blessed shalt thou be in the field.

Blessed shall be the fruit of thy body, and the fruit of thy ground, and the fruit of thy cattle, the increase of thy kine, and the flocks of thy sheep.

Blessed shall be thy basket and thy store.

Blessed shalt thou be when thou comest in, and blessed shalt thou be when thou goest out.

The Lord shall cause thine enemies that rise up against thee to be smitten before thy face: they shall come out against thee one way, and flee before thee seven ways.

The Lord shall command the blessing upon thee in thy storehouses, and in all that thou settest thine hand unto; and he shall bless thee in the land which the Lord thy God giveth thee.

Deuteronomy 28:2-8

And the Lord shall make thee plenteous in goods, in the fruit of thy body, and in the fruit of thy cattle, and in the fruit of thy ground, in the land which the Lord sware unto thy fathers to give thee.

The Lord shall open unto thee his good treasure, the heaven to give the rain unto thy land in his season, and to bless all the work of thine hand: and thou shalt lend unto many nations, and thou shalt not borrow.

And the Lord shall make thee the head, and not the tail; and thou shalt be above only, and thou shalt not be beneath; if that thou hearken unto the commandments of the Lord thy God, which I command thee this day, to observe and to do them:

Deuteronomy 28:11-13

Give, and it shall be given unto you; good measure, pressed down, and shaken together, and running over, shall men give into your bosom. For with the same measure that ye mete withal it shall be measured to you again.

Luke 6:38

Upon the first day of the week let every one of you lay by him in store, as God hath prospered him, that there be no gatherings when I come.

I Corinthians 16:2

Heal the sick, cleanse the lepers, raise the dead, cast out devils: freely ye have received, freely give.

Matthew 10:8

Bring ye all the tithes into the storehouse, that there may be meat in mine house, and prove me now herewith, saith the Lord of hosts, if I will not open you the windows of heaven, and pour you out a blessing, that there shall not be room enough to receive it.

And I will rebuke the devourer for your sakes, and he shall not destroy the fruits of your ground; neither shall your vine cast her fruit before the time in the field, saith the Lord of hosts.

And all nations shall call you blessed: for ye shall be a delightsome land, saith the Lord of hosts.

Malachi 3:10-12

But this I say, He which soweth sparingly shall reap also sparingly; and he which soweth bountifully shall reap also bountifully.

Every man according as he purposeth in his heart, so let him give; not grudgingly, or of necessity: for God loveth a cheerful giver.

And God is able to make all grace abound toward you; that ye, always having all sufficiency in all things, may abound to every good work:

II Corinthians 9:6-8

And every one that hath forsaken houses, or brethren, or sisters, or father, or mother, or wife, or children, or lands, for my name's sake, shall receive an hundredfold, and shall inherit everlasting life.

Matthew 19:29

This book of the law shall not depart out of thy mouth; but thou shalt meditate therein day and night, that thou mayest observe to do according to all that is written therein: for then thou shalt make thy way prosperous, and then thou shalt have good success.

Joshua 1:8

For God giveth to a man that is good in his sight wisdom, and knowledge, and joy: but to the sinner he giveth travail, to gather and to heap up, that he may give to him that is good before God. This also is vanity and vexation of Spirit.

Ecclesiastes 2:26

A good man leaveth an inheritance to his children's children: and the wealth of the sinner is laid up for the just.

Proverbs 13:22

For the Lord thy God bringeth thee into a good land, a land of brooks of water, of fountains and depths that spring out of valleys and hills;

A land of wheat, and barley, and vines, and fig trees, and pomegranates; a land of oil olive, and honey;

A land wherein thou shalt eat bread without scarceness, thou shalt not lack any thing in it; a land whose stones are iron, and out of whose hills thou mayest dig brass.

When thou hast eaten and art full, then thou shalt bless the Lord thy God for the good land which he hath given thee.

Beware that thou forget not the Lord thy God, in not keeping his commandments, and his judgments, and his statutes, which I command thee this day:

Lest when thou hast eaten and art full, and hast built goodly houses, and dwelt therein;

And when thy herds and thy flocks multiply, and thy silver and thy gold is multiplied, and all that thou hast is multiplied;

Then thine heart be lifted up, and thou forget the Lord thy God, which brought thee forth out of the land of Egypt, from the house of bondage;

But thou shalt remember the Lord thy God: for it is he that giveth thee power to get wealth, that he may establish his covenant which he sware unto thy fathers, as it is this day.

Deuteronomy 8:7-14,18

Therefore take no thought, saying, What shall we eat? or, What shall we drink? or, Wherewithal shall we be clothed?

(For after all these things do the Gentiles seek:) for your heavenly Father knoweth that ye have need of all these things.

But seek ye first the kingdom of God, and his righteousness; and all these things shall be added unto you.

Matthew 6:31-33

But my God shall supply all your need according to his riches in glory by Christ Jesus.

Philippians 4:19

You Are Having Marital Problems

Let all bitterness, and wrath, and anger, and clamour, and evil speaking, be put away from you, with all malice.

And be ye kind one to another, tenderhearted, forgiving one another, even as God for Christ's sake hath forgiven you.

Ephesians 4:31, 32

And the Lord God said, it is not good that the man should be alone, I will make him an help meet for him.

Genesis 2:18

Therefore shall a man leave his father and his mother, and shall cleave unto his wife: and they shall be one flesh.

Genesis 2:24

Submitting yourselves one to another in the fear of God.

Wives, submit yourselves unto your own husbands, as unto the Lord.

For the husband is the head of the wife, even as Christ is the head of the church: and he is the saviour of the body.

Therefore as the church is subject unto Christ, so let the wives be to their own husbands in every thing.

Husbands, love your wives, even as Christ also loved the church, and gave himself for it;

That he might sanctify and cleanse it with the washing of water by the word.

That he might present it to himself a glorious church, not having spot, or wrinkle, or any such thing; but that it should be holy and without blemish.

So ought men to love their wives as their own bodies. He that loveth his wife loveth himself.

For no man ever yet hated his own flesh; but nourisheth and cherisheth it, even as the Lord the church:

For we are members of his body, of his flesh, and of his bones.

For this cause shall a man leave his father and mother, and shall be joined unto his wife, and they two shall be one flesh.

This is a great mystery: but I speak concerning Christ and the church.

Nevertheless let everyone of you in particular so love his wife even as himself; and the wife see that she reverence her husband.

Ephesians 5:21-33

Likewise, ye wives, be in subjection to your own husbands; that, if any obey not the word, they also may without the word be won by the conversation of the wives,

While they behold your chaste conversation coupled with fear.

Whose adorning let it not be that outward adorning of plaiting the hair, and of wearing of gold, or of putting on of apparel;

But let it be the hidden man of the heart, in that which is not corruptible, even the ornament of a meek and quiet spirit, which is in the sight of God of great price.

For after this manner in the old time the holy women also who trusted in God, adorned themselves, being in subjection unto their own husbands:

Even as Sara obeyed Abraham, calling him lord: whose daughters ye are, as long as ye do well, and are not afraid with any amazement.

Likewise, ye husbands, dwell with them according to knowledge, giving honour unto the wife, as unto the weaker vessel and as being heirs together of the grace of life; that your prayers be not hindered.

I Peter 3:1-7

And if it seem evil unto you to serve the Lord, choose you this day whom ye will serve; whether the gods which your fathers served that were on the other side of the flood, or the gods of the Amorites, in whose land ye dwell: but as for me and my house, we will serve the Lord.

Joshua 24:15

Love worketh no ill to his neighbour: therefore love is the fulfilling of the law.

Romans 13:10

I will behave myself wisely in a perfect way. O when wilt thou come unto me? I will walk within my house with a perfect heart.

Psalm 101:2

Finally, be ye all of one mind, having compassion one of another, love as brethren, be pitiful, be courteous:

Not rendering evil for evil, or railing for railing: but contrariwise blessing; knowing that ye are thereunto called, that ye should inherit a blessing.

For he that will love life, and see good days, let him refrain his tongue from evil, and his lips that they speak no guile:

Let him eschew evil, and do good; let him seek peace, and ensue it.

I Peter 3:8-11

Trust in the Lord with all thine heart; and lean not unto thine own understanding.

In all thy ways acknowledge him, and he shall direct thy paths.

Proverbs 3:5, 6

Hatred stirreth up strifes: but love covereth all sins.

Proverbs 10:12

Seeing ye have purified your souls in obeying the truth through the Spirit unto unfeigned love of the brethren, see that ye love one another with a pure heart fervently:

I Peter 1:22

WHAT TO DO WHEN

You Are Deserted By Loved Ones

And they that know thy name will put their trust in thee: for thou, Lord, hast not forsaken them that seek thee.

Psalm 9:10

For the Lord will not cast off his people, neither will he forsake his inheritance.

Psalm 94:14

When my father and my mother forsake me, then the Lord will take me up.

Psalm 27:10

Teaching them to observe all things whatsoever I have commanded you: and, lo, I am with you alway, even unto the end of the world. Amen.

Matthew 28:20

Thou shalt no more be termed Forsaken; neither shall thy land any more be termed Desolate: but thou shalt be called Hephzibah, and thy land Beulah: for the Lord delighteth in thee, and thy land shall be married.

Isaiah 62:4

Persecuted, but not forsaken; cast down, but not destroyed;

II Corinthians 4:9

Casting all your care upon him; for he careth for you.

I Peter 5:7

I have been young, and now am old; yet have I not seen the righteous forsaken, nor his seed begging bread.

Psalm 37:25

For the Lord thy God is a merciful God; he will not forsake thee, neither destroy thee, nor forget the covenant of thy fathers which he sware unto them.

Deuteronomy 4:31

When the poor and needy seek water, and there is none, and their tongue faileth for thirst, I the Lord will hear them, I the God of Israel will not forsake them.

Isaiah 41:17

Because he hath set his love upon me, therefore will I deliver him: I will set him on high, because he hath known my name.
He shall call upon me, and I will answer him: I will be with him in trouble; I will deliver him, and honour him.

Psalm 91:14, 15

Can a woman forget her sucking child, that she should not have compassion on the son of her womb? yea, they may forget, yet will I not forget thee.

Behold, I have graven thee upon the palms of my hands; thy walls are continually before me.

Isaiah 49:15, 16

Why art thou cast down, O my soul? and why art thou disquieted within me? hope in God: for I shall yet praise him, who is the health of my countenance, and my God.

Psalm 43:5

Be strong and of a good courage, fear not, nor be afraid of them: for the Lord thy God, he it is that doth go with thee; he will not fail thee, nor forsake thee.

Deuteronomy 31:6

For the Lord will not forsake his people for his great name's sake: because it hath pleased the Lord to make you his people.

I Samuel 12:22

You Do Not Understand God's Ways

For my thoughts are not your thoughts, neither are your ways my ways, saith the Lord.

For as the heavens are higher than the earth, so are my ways higher than your ways, and my thoughts than your thoughts.

Isaiah 55:8, 9

Call unto me, and I will answer thee, and shew thee great and mighty things, which thou knowest not.

Jeremiah 33:3

What shall we then say to these things? If God be for us, who can be against us?

Romans 8:31

Who shall separate us from the love of Christ? shall tribulation, or distress, or persecution, or famine, or nakedness, or peril, or sword?

As it is written, For thy sake we are killed all the day long; we are accounted as sheep for the slaughter.

Nay, in all these things we are more than conquerors through him that loved us.

Romans 8:35-37

There hath no temptation taken you but such as is common to man: but God is faithful, who will not suffer you to be tempted above that ye are able; but will with the temptation also make a way to escape, that ye may be able to bear it.

I Corinthians 10:13

Many are the afflictions of the righteous: but the Lord delivereth him out of them all.

Psalm 34:19

Cast thy burden upon the Lord, and he shall sustain thee: he shall never suffer the righteous to be moved.

Psalm 55:22

Fear thou not; for I am with thee: be not dismayed; for I am thy God: I will strengthen thee; yea, I will help thee; yea, I will uphold thee with the right hand of my righteousness.

Isaiah 41:10

And we know that all things work together for good to them that love God, to them who are the called according to his purpose.

Romans 8:28

Then shall we know, if we follow on to know the Lord: his going forth is prepared as the morning; and he shall come unto us as the rain, as the latter and former rain unto the earth.

Hosea 6:3

As for God, his way is perfect: the word of the Lord is tried: he is a buckler to all those that trust in him.

Psalm 18:30

Let us hold fast the profession of our faith without wavering; (for he is faithful that promised;)

Hebrews 10:23

And I will make an everlasting covenant with them, that I will not turn away from them, to do them good; but I will put my fear in their hearts, that they shall not depart from me.

Jeremiah 32:40

The Lord will perfect that which concerneth me: thy mercy, O Lord, endureth for ever: forsake not the works of thine own hands.

Psalm 138:8

Beloved, think it not strange concerning the fiery trial which is to try you, as though some strange thing happened unto you:

But rejoice, inasmuch as ye are partakers of Christ's sufferings; that, when his glory shall be revealed, ye may be glad also with exceeding joy.

I Peter 4:12, 13

WHAT TO DO WHEN

Waiting On God

Wait on the Lord: be of good courage, and he shall strengthen thine heart: wait, I say, on the Lord.

Psalm 27:14

My soul, wait thou only upon God; for my expectation is from him.

Psalm 62:5

Our soul waiteth for the Lord: he is our help and our shield.

Psalm 33:20

But they that wait upon the Lord shall renew their strength; they shall mount up with wings as eagles; they shall run, and not be weary; and they shall walk, and not faint.

Isaiah 40:31

For the vision is yet for an appointed time, but at the end it shall speak, and not lie: though it tarry, wait for it; because it will surely come, it will not tarry.

Habakkuk 2:3

Let us hold fast the profession of our faith without wavering; (for he is faithful that promised;)

Hebrews 10:23

Cast not away therefore your confidence, which hath great recompence of reward.

The eyes of all wait upon thee; and thou givest them their meat in due season.

Thou openest thine hand, and satisfiest the desire of every living thing.

Psalm 145:15, 16

I wait for the Lord, my soul doth wait, and in his word do I hope.

Psalm 130:5

For we are made partakers of Christ, if we hold the beginning of our confidence stedfast unto the end;

Hebrews 3:14

And it shall be said in the day, Lo, this is our God; we have waited for him, and he will save us: this is the Lord; we have waited for him, we will be glad and rejoice in his salvation.

Isaiah 25:9

What The Bible Has To Say About . . .

Faith

Now faith is the substance of things hoped for, the evidence of things not seen.

Hebrews 11:1

So then faith cometh by hearing, and hearing by the word of God.

Romans 10:17

For I say, through the grace given unto me, to every man that is among you, not to think of himself more highly than he ought to think; but to think soberly, according as God hath dealt to every man the measure of faith.

Romans 12:3

Looking unto Jesus the author and finisher of our faith, who for the joy that was set before him endured the cross, despising the shame, and is set down at the right hand of the throne of God.

Hebrews 12:2

And Jesus said unto them, Because of your unbelief: for verily I say unto you, If ye have faith as a grain of mustard seed, ye shall say unto this mountain, Remove hence to yonder place, and it shall remove, and nothing shall be impossible unto you.

Matthew 17:20

And Jesus answering saith unto them, Have faith in God.

For verily I say unto you, That whosoever shall say unto this mountain, Be thou removed, and be thou cast into the sea; and shall not doubt in his heart, but shall believe that those things which he saith shall come to pass, he shall have whatsoever he saith.

Therefore I say unto you, What things soever ye desire, when ye pray, believe that ye receive them, and ye shall have them.

Mark 11:22-24

For therein is the righteousness of God revealed from faith to faith: as it is written, The just shall live by faith.

Romans 1:17

(For we walk by faith, not by sight:)

II Corinthians 5:7

But without faith it is impossible to please him; for he that cometh to God must believe that he is, and that he is a rewarder of them that diligently seek him.

Hebrews 11:6

That the trial of your faith, being much more precious than of gold that perisheth, though it be tried with fire, might be found unto praise and honour and glory at the appearing of Jesus Christ:

Whom having not seen, ye love; in whom, though now ye see him not, yet believing, ye rejoice with joy unspeakable and full of glory:

Receiving the end of your faith, even the salvation of your souls.

I Peter 1:7-9

For whatsoever is born of God overcometh the world: and this is the victory that overcometh the world, even our faith.

I John 5:4

And, behold, a woman, which was diseased with an issue of blood twelve years, came behind him, and touched the hem of his garment:

For she said within herself, if I may but touch his garment, I shall be whole.

But Jesus turned him about, and when he saw her, he said, Daughter, be of good comfort; thy faith hath made thee whole.

Matthew 9:20-22

And when he was come into the house, the blind men came to him: and Jesus saith unto them, Believe ye that I am able to do this? They said unto him, Yea, Lord.

Then touched he their eyes, saying, According to your faith be it unto you.

Matthew 9:28, 29

Jesus said unto him, If thou canst believe, all things are possible to him that believeth.

Mark 9:23

Is any sick among you? let him call for the elders of the church; and let them pray over him anointing him with oil in the name of the Lord:

And the prayer of faith shall save the sick, and the Lord shall raise him up,

James 5:14, 15a

Love

Beloved, let us love one another: for love is of God; and every one that loveth is born of God, and knoweth God.

He that loveth not knoweth not God; for God is love.

I John 4:7, 8

Though I speak with the tongues of men and of angels, and have not charity, I am become as sounding brass, or a tinkling cymbal.

And though I have the gift of prophecy, and understand all mysteries, and all knowledge; and though I have all faith, so that I could remove mountains, and have not charity, I am nothing.

And though I bestow all my goods to feed the poor, and though I give my body to be burned, and have not charity, it profiteth me nothing.

Charity suffereth long, and is kind; charity envieth not; charity vaunteth not itself, is not puffed up,

Doth not behave itself unseemly, seeketh not her own, is not easily provoked, thinketh no evil;

Rejoiceth not in iniquity, but rejoiceth in the truth;

Beareth all things, believeth all things, hopeth all things, endureth all things.

Charity never faileth:

And now abideth faith, hope, charity, these three; but the greatest of these is charity.

I Corinthians 13:1-8a, 13

Herein is love, not that we loved God, but that he loved us, and sent his Son to be the propitiation for our sins.

Beloved, if God so loved us, we ought also to love one another.

No man hath seen God at any time. If we love one another, God dwelleth in us, and his love is perfected in us.

I John 4:10-12

As the Father hath loved me, so have I loved you: continue ye in my love.

If ye keep my commandments, ye shall abide in my love; even as I have kept my Father's commandments, and abide in his love.

John 15:9, 10

He that hath my commandments, and keepeth them, he it is that loveth me: and he that loveth me shall be loved of my Father, and I will love him, and will manifest myself to him.

John 14:21

This is my commandment, That ye love one another, as I have loved you.

Greater love hath no man than this, that a man lay down his life for his friends.

Ye are my friends, if ye do whatsoever I command you.

These things I command you, that ye love one another.

John 15:12-14, 17

And thou shalt love the Lord thy God with all thy heart, and with all thy soul, and with all thy mind, and with all thy strength: this is the first commandment.

And the second is like, namely this, Thou shalt love thy neighbour as thyself. There is none other commandment greater than these.

And to love him with all the heart, and with all the understanding, and with all the soul, and with all the strength, and to love his neighbour as himself, is more than all whole burnt offerings and sacrifices.

Mark 12:30, 31, 33

And we have known and believed the love that God hath to us. God is love; and he that dwelleth in love dwelleth in God, and God in him.

And this commandment have we from him, That he who loveth God love his brother also.

I John 4:16, 21

The Lord hath appeared of old unto me, saying, Yea, I have loved thee with an everlasting love: therefore with loving-kindness have I drawn thee.

Jeremiah 31:3

For the Father himself loveth you, because ye have loved me, and have believed that I come out from God.

John 16:27

But God commendeth his love toward us, in that, while we were yet sinners, Christ died for us.

Romans 5:8

For God so loved the world, that he gave his only begotten Son, that whosoever believeth in him should not perish, but have everlasting life.

John 3:16

For I am persuaded, that neither death, nor life, nor angels, nor principalities, nor powers, nor things present, nor things to come,
Nor height, nor depth, nor any other creature, shall be able to separate us from the love of God, which is in Christ Jesus our Lord.

Romans 8:38, 39

A new commandment I give unto you,
That ye love one another; as I have loved
you, that ye also love one another.

By this shall all men know that ye are
my disciples, if ye have love one to another.
John 13:34, 35

Eternity

And this is the record, that God hath given to us eternal life, and this life is in his Son.

I John 5:11

Verily, verily, I say unto you, He that heareth my word, and believeth on him that sent me, hath everlasting life, and shall not come into condemnation; but is passed from death unto life.

John 5:24

For God so loved the world, that he gave his only begotten Son, that whosoever believeth in him should not perish, but have everlasting life.

John 3:16

Verily, verily, I say unto you, He that believeth on me hath everlasting life.

John 6:47

I am the living bread which came down from heaven; if any man eat of this bread, he shall live for ever: and the bread that I will give is my flesh, which I will give for the life of the world.

John 6:51

And we know that the Son of God is come, and hath given us an understanding, that we may know him that is true, and we are in him that is true, even in his Son Jesus Christ. This is the true God, and eternal life.

I John 5:20

The meek shall eat and be satisfied: they shall praise the Lord that seek him: your heart shall live for ever.

Psalm 22:26

The Lord knoweth the days of the upright: and their inheritance shall be for ever.

Psalm 37:18

Surely goodness and mercy shall follow me all the days of my life: and I will dwell in the house of the Lord for ever.

Psalm 23:6

But God will redeem my soul from the power of the grave: for he shall receive me. Selah.

Psalm 49:15

So when this corruptible shall have put on incorruption, and this mortal shall have put on immortality, then shall be brought to pass the saying that is written, Death is swallowed up in victory.

O death, where is thy sting? O grave, where is thy victory?

I Corinthians 15:54, 55

Jesus said unto her, I am the resurrection, and the life: he that believeth in me, though he were dead, yet shall he live:

And whosoever liveth and believeth in me shall never die. Believest thou this?

John 11:25, 26

Labour not for the meat which perisheth, but for that which endureth unto everlasting life, which the Son of man shall give unto you: for him hath God the Father sealed.

John 6:27

My sheep hear my voice, and I know them, and they follow me:

And I give unto them eternal life; and they shall never perish, neither shall any man pluck them out of my hand.

John 10:27, 28

But whosoever drinketh of the water that I shall give him shall never thirst; but the water that I shall give him shall be in him a well of water springing up into everlasting life.

John 4:14

Praise

This people have I formed for myself; they shall shew forth my praise.

Isaiah 43:21

But ye are a chosen generation, a royal priesthood, an holy nation, a peculiar people; that ye should shew forth the praises of him who hath called you out of darkness into his marvellous light:

I Peter 2:9

By him therefore let us offer the sacrifice of praise to God continually, that is, the fruit of our lips giving thanks to his name.

Hebrews 13:15

Praise ye the Lord: for it is good to sing praises unto our God; for it is pleasant; and praise is comely.

Psalms 147:1

I will call on the Lord, who is worthy to be praised: so shall I be saved from mine enemies.

II Samuel 22:4

I will bless the Lord at all times: his praise shall continually be in my mouth.

Psalm 34:1

O Clap your hands, all ye people; shout unto God with the voice of triumph.

Sing praises to God, sing praises: sing praises unto our King, sing praises.

For God is the King of all the earth: sing ye praises with understanding.

Psalm 47:1, 6, 7

Great is the Lord, and greatly to be praised in the city of our God, in the mountain of his holiness.

Psalm 48:1

Whoso offereth praise glorifieth me: and to him that ordereth his conversation aright will I shew the salvation of God.

Psalm 50:23

Because thy lovingkindness is better than life, my lips shall praise thee.

Thus will I bless thee while I live: I will lift up my hands in thy name.

My soul shall be satisfied as with marrow and fatness; and my mouth shall praise thee with joyful lips:

Psalm 63:3-5

Let my mouth be filled with thy praise and with thy honour all the day. But I will hope continually, and will yet praise thee more and more.

Psalm 71:8, 14

It is a good thing to give thanks unto the Lord, and to sing praises unto thy name, O most High:

Psalm 92:1

For the Lord is great, and greatly to be praised:

Psalm 96:4a

Oh that men would praise the Lord for his goodness, and for his wonderful works to the children of men!

Psalm 107:8

And at midnight Paul and Silas prayed, and sang praises unto God: and the prisoners heard them.

Acts 16:25

And be not drunk with wine, wherein is excess; but be filled with the Spirit;

Speaking to yourselves in psalms and hymns and spiritual songs, singing and making melody in your heart to the Lord;

Giving thanks always for all things unto God the Father in the name of our Lord Jesus Christ;

Ephesians 5:18-20

Serving God

Ye shall walk after the Lord your God, and fear him, and keep his commandments, and obey his voice, and ye shall serve him, and cleave unto him.

Deuteronomy 13:4

No man can serve two masters: for either he will hate the one, and love the other; or else he will hold to the one, and despise the other. Ye cannot serve God and mammon.

Matthew 6:24

Then saith Jesus unto him, Get thee hence, Satan: for it is written, Thou shalt worship the Lord thy God, and him only shalt thou serve.

Matthew 4:10

But take diligent heed to do the commandment and the law, which Moses the servant of the Lord charged you, to love the Lord your God, and to walk in all his ways, and to keep his commandments, and to cleave unto him, and to serve him with all your heart and with all your soul.

Joshua 22:5

I beseech you therefore, brethren, by the mercies of God, that ye present your bodies a living sacrifice, holy, acceptable unto God, which is your reasonable service.

And be not conformed to this world: but be ye transformed by the renewing of your mind, that ye may prove what is that good, and acceptable, and perfect, will of God.

Romans 12:1, 2

Be kindly affectioned one to another with brotherly love; in honour preferring one another;

Not slothful in business; fervent in spirit; serving the Lord;

Distributing to the necessity of saints; given to hospitality.

Romans 12:10, 11, 13

And ye shall serve the Lord your God, and he shall bless thy bread, and thy water; and I will take sickness away from the midst of thee.

There shall nothing cast their young, nor be barren, in thy land: the number of thy days I will fulfil.

Exodus 23:25, 26

And now, Israel, what doth the Lord thy God require of thee, but to fear the Lord thy God, to walk in all his ways, and to love him, and to serve the Lord thy God with all thy heart and with all thy soul,

Deuteronomy 10:12

And it shall come to pass, if ye shall hearken diligently unto my commandments which I command you this day, to love the Lord your God, and to serve him with all your heart and with all your soul,

That I will give you the rain of your land in his due season, the first rain and the latter rain, that thou mayest gather in thy corn, and thy wine, and thine oil.

And I will send grass in thy fields for thy cattle, that thou mayest eat and be full.

Deuteronomy 11:13-15

And if it seem evil unto you to serve the Lord, choose you this day whom ye will serve; whether the gods which your fathers served that were on the other side of the flood, or the gods of the Amorites, in whose land ye dwell: but as for me and my house, we will serve the Lord.

Joshua 24:15

And Samuel said unto the people, Fear not: ye have done all this wickedness: yet turn not aside from following the Lord, but serve the Lord with all your heart;

And turn ye not aside: for then should ye go after vain things, which cannot profit nor deliver; for they are vain.

For the Lord will not forsake his people for his great name's sake: because it hath pleased the Lord to make you his people.

I Samuel 12:20-22

And thou, Solomon my son, know thou the God of thy father, and serve him with a perfect heart and with a willing mind: for the Lord searcheth all hearts, and understandeth all the imaginations of the thoughts: if thou seek him, he will be found of thee; but if thou forsake him, he will cast thee off for ever.

I Chronicles 28:9

But now we are delivered from the law, that being dead wherein we were held; that we should serve in newness of spirit, and not in the oldness of the letter.

Romans 7:6

Make a joyful noise unto the Lord, all ye lands.

Serve the Lord with gladness: come before his presence with singing.

Enter into his gates with thanksgiving, and into his courts with praise: be thankful unto him, and bless his name.

Psalm 100:1, 2, 4

Obedience

Behold, I set before you this day a blessing and a curse;

A blessing, if ye obey the commandments of the Lord your God, which I command you this day:

And a curse, if ye will not obey the commandments of the Lord your God, but turn aside out of the way which I command you this day, to go after other gods, which ye have not known.

Deuteronomy 11:26-28

And Samuel said, Hath the Lord as great delight in burnt offerings and sacrifices, as in obeying the voice of the Lord? Behold, to obey is better than sacrifice, and to hearken than the fat of rams.

I Samuel 15:22

O that thou hadst hearkened to my commandments! then had thy peace been as a river, and thy righteousness as the waves of the sea:

Isaiah 48:18

But this thing commanded I them, saying, Obey my voice, and I will be your God, and ye shall be my people: and walk ye in all the ways that I have commanded you, that it may be well unto you.

Jeremiah 7:23

If ye shall ask any thing in my name, I will do it.

He that hath my commandments, and keepeth them, he it is that loveth me: and he that loveth me shall be loved of my Father, and I will love him, and will manifest myself to him.

John 14:15, 21

Then Peter and the other apostles answered and said, We ought to obey God rather than men.

Acts 5:29

And hereby we do know that we know him, if we keep his commandments.

He that saith, I know him, and keepeth not his commandments, is a liar, and the truth is not in him.

But whoso keepeth his word, in him verily is the love of God perfected: hereby know we that we are in him.

He that saith he abideth in him ought himself also so to walk, even as he walked.

I John 2:3-6

And if thou wilt walk in my ways, to keep my statutes and my commandments, as thy father David did walk, then I will lengthen thy days.

I Kings 3:14

Teach me to do thy will; for thou art my God: thy spirit is good; lead me into the land of uprightness.

Psalm 143:10

And Moses called all Israel, and said unto them, Hear, O Israel, the statutes and judgments which I speak in your ears this day, that ye may learn them, and keep, and do them.

Ye shall observe to do therefore as the Lord your God hath commanded you: ye shall not turn aside to the right hand or to the left.

Ye shall walk in all the ways which the Lord your God hath commanded you, that ye may live, and that it may be well with you, and that ye may prolong your days in the land which ye shall possess.

Deuteronomy 5:1, 32, 33

Servants, obey in all things your masters according to the flesh; not with eye-service, as menpleasers; but in singleness of heart, fearing God:

And whatsoever ye do, do it heartily, as to the Lord, and not unto men;

Knowing that of the Lord ye shall receive the reward of the inheritance: for ye serve the Lord Christ.

Colossians 3:22-24

Submit yourselves to every ordinance of man for the Lord's sake: whether it be to the king, as supreme;

Or unto governors, as unto them that are sent by him for the punishment of evildoers, and for the praise of them that do well.

For so is the will of God, that with well-doing ye may put to silence the ignorance of foolish men:

As free, and not using your liberty for a cloak of maliciousness, but as the servants of God.

Honour all men. Love the brotherhood. Fear God. Honour the king.

Servants, be subject to your masters with all fear; not only to the good and gentle, but also to the froward.

For this is thankworthy, if a man for conscience toward God endure grief, suffering wrongfully.

For what glory is it, if, when ye be buffeted for your faults, ye shall take it patiently? but if, when ye do well, and suffer for it, ye take it patiently, this is acceptable with God.

I Peter 2:13-20

Children, obey your parents in the Lord: for this is right.

Ephesians 6:1

Children, obey your parents in all things: for this is well pleasing unto the Lord.

Fathers, provoke not your children to anger, lest they be discouraged.

Servants, obey in all things your masters according to the flesh; not with eye-service, as menpleasers; but in singleness of heart, fearing God:

And whatsoever ye do, do it heartily, as to the Lord, and not unto men;

Knowing that of the Lord ye shall receive the reward of the inheritance: for ye serve the Lord Christ.

Colossians 3:20-24

WHAT THE BIBLE HAS TO SAY ABOUT
The Carnal Mind

For to be carnally minded is death; but to be spiritually minded is life and peace.

Because the carnal mind is enmity against God: for it is not subject to the law of God, neither indeed can be.

So then they that are in the flesh cannot please God.

Romans 8:6-8

For he that soweth to his flesh shall of the flesh reap corruption, but he that soweth to the Spirit shall of the Spirit reap life everlasting.

Galatians 6:8

Ye adulterers and adulteresses, know ye not that the friendship of the world is enmity with God? whosoever therefore will be a friend of the world is the enemy of God.

James 4:4

There is a way which seemeth right unto a man, but the end thereof are the ways of death.

Proverbs 14:12

(For many walk, of whom I have told you often, and now tell you even weeping, that they are the enemies of the cross of Christ:

Whose end is destruction, whose God is their belly, and whose glory is in their shame, who mind earthly things.)

Philippians 3:18, 19

But she that liveth in pleasure is dead while she liveth.

I Timothy 5:6

No man that warreth entangleth himself with the affairs of this life; that he may please him who hath chosen him to be a soldier.

Flee also youthful lusts: but follow righteousness, faith, charity, peace, with them that call on the Lord out of a pure heart.

II Timothy 2:4, 22

For men shall be lovers of their own selves, covetous, boasters, proud, blasphemers, disobedient to parents, unthankful, unholy,

Without natural affection, truce-breakers, false accusers, incontinent, fierce, despisers of those that are good,

Traitors, heady, highminded, lovers of pleasure more than lovers of God;

Having a form of godliness, but denying the power thereof: from such turn away.

For of this sort are they which creep into houses, and lead captive silly women laden with sins, led away with divers lusts,

Ever learning, and never able to come to the knowledge of the truth.

II Timothy 3:2-7

Dearly beloved, I beseech you as strangers and pilgrims, abstain from fleshly lusts, which war against the soul;

I Peter 2:11

Love not the world, neither the things that are in the world, If any man love the world, the love of the Father is not in him.

For all that is in the world, the lust of the flesh, and the lust of the eyes, and the pride of life, is not of the Father, but is of the world.

And the world passeth away, and the lust thereof: but he that doeth the will of God abideth for ever.

I John 2:15-17

I beseech you therefore, brethren, by the mercies of God, that ye present your bodies a living sacrifice, holy, acceptable unto God, which is your reasonable service.

And be not conformed to this world: but be ye transformed by the renewing of your mind, that ye may prove what is that good, and acceptable, and perfect, will of God.

Romans 12:1, 2

Let this mind be in you, which was also in Christ Jesus.

Philippians 2:5

Thou wilt keep him in perfect peace, whose mind is stayed on thee: because he trusteth in thee.

Isaiah 26:3

Set your affection on things above, not on things on the earth.

Mortify therefore your members which are upon the earth; fornication, uncleanness, inordinate affection, evil concupiscence, and covetousness, which is idolatry:

Colossians 3:2, 5

Finally, brethren, whatsoever things are true, whatsoever things are honest, whatsoever things are just, whatsoever things are pure, whatsoever things are lovely, whatsoever things are of good report; if there be any virtue, and if there be any praise, think on these things.

Philippians 4:8

The Grace Of God

And with great power gave the apostles witness of the resurrection of the Lord Jesus: and great grace was upon them all.

Acts 4:33

So shalt thou find favour and good understanding in the sight of God and man.

Proverbs 3:4

For the Lord God is a sun and shield: the Lord will give grace and glory: no good thing will he withhold from them that walk uprightly.

Psalm 84:11

And the Lord said unto Moses, I will do this thing also that thou hast spoken: for thou hast found grace in my sight, and I know thee by name.

Exodus 33:17

Thou hast granted me life and favour, and thy visitation hath preserved my spirit.

Job 10:12

For thou, Lord, wilt bless the righteous; with favour wilt thou compass him as with a shield.

Psalm 5:12

Lord, by thy favour thou hast made my mountain to stand strong: thou didst hide thy face, and I was troubled.

Psalm 30:7

The Lord hath been mindful of us: he will bless us; he will bless the house of Israel; he will bless the house of Aaron.

He will bless them that fear the Lord, both small and great.

Psalm 115:12, 13

For whoso findeth me findeth life, and shall obtain favour of the Lord.

Proverbs 8:35

Blessings are upon the head of the just: but violence covereth the mouth of the wicked.

The blessing of the Lord, it maketh rich, and he addeth no sorrow with it.

The fear of the wicked, it shall come upon him: but the desire of the righteous shall be granted.

Proverbs 10:6, 22, 24

Fools make a mock at sin: but among the righteous there is favour.

Proverbs 14:9

And the sons of strangers shall build up thy walls, and their kings shall minister unto thee: for in my wrath I smote thee, but in my favour have I had mercy on thee.

Isaiah 60:10

For all things are for your sakes, that the abundant grace might through the thanksgiving of many redound to the glory of God.

II Corinthians 4:15

To the praise of the glory of his grace, wherein he hath made us accepted in the beloved.

Ephesians 1:6

Let us therefore come boldly unto the throne of grace, that we may obtain mercy, and find grace to help in time of need.

Hebrews 4:16

The Holy Spirit

What? know ye not that your body is the temple of the Holy Ghost which is in you, which ye have of God, and ye are not your own?

I Corinthians 6:19

And hope maketh not ashamed; because the love of God is shed abroad in our hearts by the Holy Ghost which is given unto us.

Romans 5:5

And I will pray the Father, and he shall give you another Comforter, that he may abide with you for ever;

Even the Spirit of truth; whom the world cannot receive, because it seeth him not, neither knoweth him: but ye know him; for he dwelleth with you, and shall be in you.

John 14:16, 17

Nevertheless I tell you the truth; It is expedient for you that I go away: for if I go not away, the Comforter will not come unto you; but if I depart, I will send him unto you.

Howbeit when he, the Spirit of truth, is come, he will guide you into all truth: for he shall not speak of himself; but whatsoever he shall hear, that shall he speak: and he will shew you things to come.

John 16:7, 13

I indeed baptize you with water unto repentance: but he that cometh after me is mightier than I, whose shoes I am not worthy to bear: he shall baptize you with the Holy Ghost, and with fire:

Matthew 3:11

He that believeth on me, as the scripture hath said, out of his belly shall flow rivers of living water.

(But this spake he of the Spirit, which they that believe on him should receive: for the Holy Ghost was not yet given; because that Jesus was not yet glorified.)

John 7:38, 39

If ye then, being evil, know how to give good gifts unto your children: how much more shall your heavenly Father give the Holy Spirit to them that ask him?

Luke 11:13

And it shall come to pass afterward, that I will pour out my spirit upon all flesh; and your sons and your daughters shall prophesy, your old men shall dream dreams, your young men shall see visions:

Joel 2:28

And, being assembled together with them, commanded them that they should not depart from Jerusalem, but wait for the promise of the Father, which, saith he, ye have heard of me.

For John truly baptized with water; but ye shall be baptized with the Holy Ghost not many days hence.

But ye shall receive power, after that the Holy Ghost is come upon you: and ye shall be witnesses unto me both in Jerusalem, and in all Judaea, and in Samaria, and unto the uttermost part of the earth.

Acts 1:4, 5, 8

And they were all filled with the Holy Ghost, and began to speak with other tongues, as the Spirit gave them utterance.

Acts 2:4

Then Peter said unto them, Repent, and be baptized every one of you in the name of Jesus Christ for the remission of sins, and ye shall receive the gift of the Holy Ghost.

Acts 2:38

And when they had prayed, the place was shaken where they were assembled together; and they were all filled with the Holy Ghost, and they spake the word of God with boldness.

Acts 4:31

And be not drunk with wine, wherein is excess; but be filled with the Spirit;

Ephesians 5:18

Now when the apostles which were at Jerusalem heard that Samaria had received the word of God, they sent unto them Peter and John:

Who, when they were come down, prayed for them, that they might receive the Holy Ghost:

(For as yet he was fallen upon none of them: only they were baptized in the name of the Lord Jesus).

Then laid they their hands on them, and they received the Holy Ghost.

Acts 8:14-17

While Peter yet spake these words, the Holy Ghost fell on all them which heard the word.

And they of the circumcision which believed were astonished, as many came with Peter, because that on the Gentiles also was poured out the gift of the Holy Ghost.

For they heard them speak with tongues, and magnify God.

Acts 10:44-46a

He said unto them, Have ye received the Holy Ghost since ye believed? And they said unto him, We have not so much as heard whether there be any Holy Ghost.

And he said unto them, Unto what then were ye baptized? And they said, Unto John's baptism.

Then said Paul, John verily baptized with the baptism of repentance, saying unto the people, that they should believe on him which should come after him, that is, on Christ Jesus.

When they heard this, they were baptized in the name of the Lord Jesus.

And when Paul had laid his hands upon them, the Holy Ghost came on them; and they spake with tongues, and prophesied.

Acts 19:2-6

WHAT THE BIBLE HAS TO SAY ABOUT
God's Faithfulness

Thou hast dealt well with thy servant,
O Lord, according unto thy word.

Psalm 119:65

Faithful is he that calleth you, who
also will do it.

I Thessalonians 5:24

For this is as the waters of Noah unto
me: for as I have sworn that the waters of
Noah should no more go over the earth; so
have I sworn that I would not be wroth with
thee, nor rebuke thee.

For the mountains shall depart, and
the hills be removed; but my kindness shall
not depart from thee, neither shall the covenant of my peace be removed, saith the Lord
that hath mercy on thee.

Isaiah 54:9, 10

And the bow shall be in the cloud; and
I will look upon it, that I may remember that
everlasting covenant between God and every
living creature of all flesh that is upon the
earth.

Genesis 9:16

And, behold, I am with thee, and will keep thee in all places whither thou goest, and will bring thee again into this land; for I will not leave thee, until I have done that which I have spoken to thee of.

Genesis 28:15

But because the Lord loved you, and because he would keep the oath which he had sworn unto your fathers, hath the Lord brought you out with a mighty hand, and redeemed you out of the house of bondmen, from the hand of Pharaoh king of Egypt.

Know therefore that the Lord thy God, he is God, the faithful God, which keepeth covenant and mercy with them that love him and keep his commandments to a thousand generations;

Deuteronomy 7:8, 9

And, behold, this day I am going the way of all the earth: and ye know in all your hearts and in all your souls, that not one thing hath failed of all the good things which the Lord your God spake concerning you; all are come to pass unto you, and not one thing hath failed thereof.

Joshua 23:14

Blessed be the Lord, that hath given rest unto his people Israel, according to all that he promised: there hath not failed one word of all his good promise, which he promised by the hand of Moses his servant.

I Kings 8:56

Thy mercy, O Lord, is in the heavens; and thy faithfulness reacheth unto the clouds.

Psalm 36:5

I will sing of the mercies of the Lord for ever: with my mouth will I make known thy faithfulness to all generations.

For I have said, Mercy shall be built up for ever: thy faithfulness shalt thou establish in the very heavens.

Nevertheless my lovingkindness will I not utterly take from him, nor suffer my faithfulness to fail.

My covenant will I not break, nor alter the thing that is gone out of my lips.

Psalm 89:1, 2, 33, 34

He will not suffer thy foot to be moved: he that keepeth thee will not slumber.

Behold, he that keepeth Israel shall neither slumber nor sleep.

Psalm 121:3, 4

God is faithful, by whom ye were called unto the fellowship of his Son Jesus Christ our Lord.

I Corinthians 1:9

There hath no temptation taken you but such as is common to man: but God is faithful, who will not suffer you to be tempted above that ye are able; but will with the temptation also make a way to escape, that ye may be able to bear it.

I Corinthians 10:13

The Lord is not slack concerning his promise, as some men count slackness; but is longsuffering to us-ward, not willing that any should perish, but that all should come to repentance.

II Peter 3:9

If we believe not, yet he abideth faithful: he cannot deny himself.
Nevertheless the foundation of God standeth sure, having this seal, The Lord knoweth them that are his. And, Let every one that nameth the name of Christ depart from iniquity.

II Timothy 2:13, 19

The Church

That in the dispensation of the fulness of times he might gather together in one all things in Christ, both which are in heaven, and which are on earth; even in him:

And hath put all things under his feet, and gave him to be the head over all things to the church,

Which is his body, the fulness of him that filleth all in all.

Ephesians 1:10, 22-23

Who hath delivered us from the power of darkness, and hath translated us into the kingdom of his dear Son:

And he is the head of the body, the church: who is the beginning, the firstborn from the dead; that in all things he might have the preeminence.

Colossians 1:13, 18

He saith unto them, But whom say ye that I am?

And Simon Peter answered and said, Thou art the Christ, the Son of the living God.

And Jesus answered and said unto him, Blessed art thou, Simon Barjona: for flesh and blood hath not revealed it unto thee, but my Father which is in heaven.

And I say also unto thee, That thou art Peter, and upon this rock I will build my church; and the gates of hell shall not prevail against it.

Matthew 16:15-18

And are built upon the foundation of the apostles and prophets, Jesus Christ himself being the chief corner stone;

In whom all the building fitly framed together groweth unto an holy temple in the Lord:

In whom ye also are builded together for an habitation of God through the Spirit.

Ephesians 2:20-22

Of whom the whole family in heaven and earth is named,

Unto him be glory in the church by Christ Jesus throughout all ages, world without end. Amen.

Ephesians 3:15, 21

For the husband is the head of the wife, even as Christ is the head of the church: and he is the saviour of the body.

Therefore as the church is subject unto Christ, so let the wives be to their own husbands in every thing.

Husbands, love your wives, even as Christ also loved the church, and gave himself for it;

That he might sanctify and cleanse it with the washing of water by the word,

That he might present it to himself a glorious church, not having spot, or wrinkle, or any such thing; but that it should be holy and without blemish.

For no man ever yet hated his own flesh; but nourisheth and cherisheth it, even as the Lord the church:

Ephesians 5:23-27, 29

And ye are complete in him, which is the head of all principality and power:

And not holding the Head, from which all the body by joints and bands having nourishment ministered, and knit together, increaseth with the increase of God.

Colossians 2:10, 19

For as we have many members in one body, and all members have not the same office:

So we, being many, are one body in Christ, and every one members one of another.

Romans 12:4, 5

For as the body is one, and hath many members, and all the members of that one body, being many, are one body: so also is Christ.

For by one Spirit are we all baptized into one body, whether we be Jews or Gentiles, whether we be bond or free; and have been all made to drink into one Spirit.

For the body is not one member, but many.

If the foot shall say, Because I am not the hand, I am not of the body; is it therefore not of the body?

And if the ear shall say, Because I am not the eye, I am not of the body; is it therefore not of the body?

If the whole body were an eye, where were the hearing? If the whole were hearing, where were the smelling?

But now hath God set the members every one of them in the body, as it hath pleased him.

And if they were all one member, where were the body?

But now are they many members, yet but one body.

And the eye cannot say unto the hand, I have no need of thee: nor again the head to the feet, I have no need of you.

Nay, much more those members of the body, which seem to be more feeble, are necessary:

And those members of the body, which we think to be less honourable, upon these we bestow more abundant honour: and our uncomely parts have more abundant comeliness.

For our comely parts have no need: but God hath tempered the body together, having given more abundant honour to that part which lacked:

That there should be no schism in the body; but that the members should have the same care one for another.

And whether one member suffer, all the members suffer with it; or one member be honoured, all the members rejoice with it.

Now ye are the body of Christ, and members in particular.

And God hath set some in the church, first apostles, secondarily prophets, thirdly teachers, after that miracles, then gifts of healings, helps, governments, diversities of tongues.

I Corinthians 12:12-28

And we beseech you, brethren, to know them which labour among you, and are over you in the Lord, and admonish you;

And to esteem them very highly in love for their work's sake. And be at peace among yourselves.

I Thessalonians 5:12, 13

Remember them which have the rule over you, who have spoken unto you the word of God: whose faith follow, considering the end of their conversation.

Obey them that have the rule over you, and submit yourselves: for they watch for your souls, as they that must give account, that they may do it with joy, and not with grief: for that is unprofitable for you.

Hebrews 13:7, 17

And he gave some, apostles; and some, prophets; and some, evangelists; and some, pastors and teachers;

For the perfecting of the saints, for the work of the ministry, for the edifying of the body of Christ:

Ephesians 4:11, 12

Then they that gladly received his word were baptized: and the same day there were added unto them about three thousand souls.

And they continued stedfastly in the apostles' doctrine and fellowship, and in breaking of bread, and in prayers.

And fear came upon every soul: and many wonders and signs were done by the apostles.

And all that believed were together, and had all things common;

And sold their possessions and goods, and parted them to all men, as every man had need.

And they, continuing daily with one accord in the temple, and breaking bread from house to house, did eat their meat with gladness and singleness of heart.

Praising God, and having favour with all the people. And the Lord added to the church daily such as should be saved.

Acts 2:41-47

Behold, how good and how pleasant it is for brethren to dwell together in unity!

Psalm 133:1

Stewardship

Will a man rob God? Yet ye have robbed me. But ye say, Wherein have we robbed thee? In tithes and offerings.

Ye are cursed with a curse: for ye have robbed me, even this whole nation.

Bring ye all the tithes into the storehouse, that there may be meat in mine house, and prove me now herewith, saith the Lord of hosts, if I will not open you the windows of heaven, and pour you out a blessing, that there shall not be room enough to receive it.

And I will rebuke the devourer for your sakes, and he shall not destroy the fruits of your ground; neither shall your vine cast her fruit before the time in the field, saith the Lord of hosts.

And all nations shall call you blessed: for ye shall be a delightsome land, saith the Lord of hosts.

Malachi 3:8-12

Now concerning the collection for the saints, as I have given order to the churches of Galatia, even so do ye.

Upon the first day of the week let every one of you lay by him in store, as God hath prospered him,

I Corinthians 16:1, 2a

But this I say, He which soweth sparingly shall reap also sparingly; and he which soweth bountifully shall reap also bountifully.

Every man according as he purposeth in his heart, so let him give, not grudgingly, or of necessity: for God loveth a cheerful giver.

And God is able to make all grace abound toward you; that ye, always having all sufficiency in all things, may abound to every good work:

II Corinthians 9:6-8

And whatsoever ye do, do it heartily, as to the Lord, and not unto men;

Knowing that of the Lord ye shall receive the reward of the inheritance: for ye serve the Lord Christ.

Colossians 3:23, 24

But lay up for yourselves treasures in heaven, where neither moth nor rust doth corrupt, and where thieves do not break through nor steal:

For where your treasure is, there will your heart be also.

Matthew 6:20, 21

Give, and it shall be given unto you; good measure, pressed down, and shaken together, and running over, shall men give into your bosom. For with the same measure that ye mete withal it shall be measured to you again.

Luke 6:38

Beloved, I wish above all things that thou mayest prosper and be in health, even as thy soul prospereth.

III John 2

But seek ye first the kingdom of God, and his righteousness; and all these things shall be added unto you.

Matthew 6:33

And every one that hath forsaken houses, or brethren, or sisters, or father, or mother, or wife, or children, or lands, for my name's sake, shall receive an hundred-fold, and shall inherit everlasting life.

Matthew 19:29

Heal the sick, cleanse the lepers, raise the dead, cast out devils: freely ye have received, freely give.

Matthew 10:8

And all these blessings shall come on thee, and overtake thee, if thou shalt hearken unto the voice of the Lord thy God.

Blessed shalt thou be in the city, and blessed shalt thou be in the field.

Blessed shall be the fruit of thy body, and the fruit of thy ground, and the fruit of thy cattle, the increase of thy kine, and the flocks of thy sheep.

Blessed shall be thy basket and thy store.

Blessed shalt thou be when thou comest in, and blessed shalt thou be when thou goest out.

The Lord shall cause thine enemies that rise up against thee to be smitten before thy face: they shall come out against thee one way, and flee before thee seven ways.

The Lord shall command the blessing upon thee in thy storehouses, and in all that thou settest thine hand unto; and he shall bless thee in the land which the Lord thy God giveth thee.

And the Lord shall make thee plenteous in goods, in the fruit of thy body, and in the fruit of thy cattle, and in the fruit of thy ground, in the land which the Lord sware unto thy fathers to give thee.

The Lord shall open unto thee his good treasure, the heaven to give the rain unto thy land in his season, and to bless all the work of thine hand: and thou shalt lend unto many nations, and thou shalt not borrow.

Deuteronomy 28:2-8, 11, 12

Keep therefore the words of this covenant, and do them, that ye may prosper in all that ye do.

Deuteronomy 29:9

Then shalt thou prosper, if thou takest heed to fulfil the statutes and judgments which the Lord charged Moses with concerning Israel:

I Chronicles 22:13a

If they obey and serve him, they shall spend their days in prosperity, and their years in pleasures.

Job 36:11

There is that scattereth, and yet increaseth; and there is that withholdeth more than is meet, but it tendeth to poverty.
The liberal soul shall be made fat: and he that watereth shall be watered also himself.

Proverbs 11:24, 25

And Jesus answered and said, Verily I say unto you, There is no man that hath left house, or brethren, or sisters, or father, or mother, or wife, or children, or lands, for my sake, and the gospel's,

But he shall receive an hundredfold now in this time, houses, and brethren, and sisters, and mothers, and children, and lands, with persecutions; and in the world to come eternal life.

Mark 10:29, 30

This book of the law shall not depart out of thy mouth; but thou shalt meditate therein day and night, that thou mayest observe to do according to all that is written therein: for then thou shalt make thy way prosperous, and then thou shalt have good success.

Joshua 1:8

Satan

Be sober, be vigilant; because your adversary the devil, as a roaring lion, walketh about, seeking whom he may devour:

Whom resist stedfast in the faith,
I Peter 5:8, 9a

Submit yourselves therefore to God. Resist the devil, and he will flee from you.
James 4:7

Finally, my brethren, be strong in the Lord, and in the power of his might.

Put on the whole armour of God, that ye may be able to stand against the wiles of the devil.

For we wrestle not against flesh and blood, but against principalities, against powers, against the rulers of the darkness of this world, against spiritual wickedness in high places.

Wherefore take unto you the whole armour of God, that ye may be able to withstand in the evil day, and having done all, to stand.

Stand therefore, having your loins girt about with truth, and having on the breastplate of righteousness;

And your feet shod with the preparation of the gospel of peace;

Above all, taking the shield of faith, wherewith ye shall be able to quench all the fiery darts of the wicked.

And take the helmet of salvation, and the sword of the Spirit, which is the word of God:

Praying always with all prayer and supplication in the Spirit, and watching thereunto with all perseverance and supplication for all saints;

Ephesians 6:10-18

But we see Jesus, who was made a little lower than the angels for the suffering of death, crowned with glory and honour; that he by the grace of God should taste death, for every man.

Forasmuch then as the children are partakers of flesh and blood, he also himself likewise took part of the same; that through death he might destroy him that had the power of death, that is, the devil;

And deliver them whom through fear of death were all their lifetime subject to bondage.

Hebrews 2:9, 14, 15

And ye are complete in him, which is the head of all principality and power:

And having spoiled principalities and

powers, he made a shew of them openly, triumphing over them in it.

Colossians 2:10, 15

Who hath delivered us from the power of darkness, and hath translated us into the kingdom of his dear Son:

Colossians 1:13

And they overcame him by the blood of the Lamb, and by the word of their testimony, and they loved not their lives unto the death.

Revelation 12:11

Beloved, believe not every spirit, but try the spirits whether they are of God: because many false prophets are gone out into the world.

Hereby know ye the Spirit of God: Every spirit that confesseth that Jesus Christ is come in the flesh is of God:

And every spirit that confesseth not that Jesus Christ is come in the flesh is not of God: and this is that spirit of antichrist, whereof ye have heard that it should come; and even now already is it in the world.

Ye are of God, little children, and have overcome them: because greater is he that is in you, than he that is in the world.

I John 4:1-4

And the seventy returned again with joy, saying, Lord, even the devils are subject unto us through thy name.

And he said unto them, I beheld Satan as lightning fall from heaven.

Behold, I give unto you power to tread on serpents and scorpions, and over all the power of the enemy: and nothing shall by any means hurt you.

Luke 10:17-19

And these signs shall follow them that believe; In my name shall they cast out devils; they shall speak with new tongues;

They shall take up serpents; and if they drink any deadly thing, it shall not hurt them; they shall lay hands on the sick, and they shall recover.

Mark 16:17, 18

But if I cast out devils by the Spirit of God, then the kingdom of God is come unto you.

Or else how can one enter into a strong man's house, and spoil his goods, except he first bind the strong man? and then he will spoil his house.

Matthew 12: 28, 29

For though we walk in the flesh, we do not war after the flesh:

(For the weapons of our warfare are not carnal, but mighty through God to the pulling down of strong holds;)

Casting down imaginations, and every high thing that exalteth itself against the knowledge of God, and bringing into captivity every thought to the obedience of Christ;

II Corinthians 10:3-5

The name of the Lord is a strong tower: the righteous runneth into it, and is safe.

Proverbs 18:10

He that committeth sin is of the devil; for the devil sinneth from the beginning. For this purpose the Son of God was manifested, that he might destroy the works of the devil.

I John 3:8

And the God of peace shall bruise Satan under your feet shortly. The grace of our Lord Jesus Christ be with you. Amen.

Romans 16:20

I write unto you, fathers, because ye have known him that is from the beginning. I write unto you, young men, because ye have overcome the wicked one. I write unto you, little children, because ye have known the Father.

I have written unto you, fathers, because ye have known him that is from the beginning. I have written unto you, young men, because ye are strong, and the word of God abideth in you, and ye have overcome the wicked one.

I John 2:13, 14

The Return Of Christ

But I would not have you to be ignorant, brethren, concerning them which
are asleep, that ye sorrow not, even as others
which have no hope.

For if we believe that Jesus died and
rose again, even so them also which sleep in
Jesus will God bring with him.

For this we say unto you by the word
of the Lord, that we which are alive and remain unto the coming of the Lord shall not
prevent them which are asleep.

For the Lord himself shall descend
from heaven with a shout, with the voice of
the archangel, and with the trump of God:
and the dead in Christ shall rise first:

Then we which are alive and remain
shall be caught up together with them in the
clouds, to meet the Lord in the air: and so
shall we ever be with the Lord.

Wherefore comfort one another with
these words.

I Thessalonians 4:13-18

Behold, I shew you a mystery; We shall
not all sleep, but we shall all be changed,

In a moment, in the twinkling of an
eye, at the last trump: for the trumpet shall
sound, and the dead shall be raised incorruptible, and we shall be changed.

For this corruptible must put on incorruption, and this mortal must put on immortality.

So when this corruptible shall have put on incorruption, and this mortal shall have put on immortality, then shall be brought to pass the saying that is written, Death is swallowed up in victory.

O death, where is thy sting? O grave, where is thy victory?

The sting of death is sin; and the strength of sin is the law.

But thanks be to God, which giveth us the victory through our Lord Jesus Christ.

I Corinthians 15:51-57

Which also said, Ye men of Galilee, why stand ye gazing up into heaven? this same Jesus, which is taken up from you into heaven, shall so come in like manner as ye have seen him go into heaven.

Acts 1:11

Looking for that blessed hope, and the glorious appearing of the great God and our Saviour Jesus Christ;

Titus 2:13

Knowing this first, that there shall come in the last days scoffers, walking after their own lusts,

And saying, Where is the promise of his coming? for since the fathers fell asleep, all things continue as they were from the beginning of the creation.

But, beloved, be not ignorant of this one thing, that one day is with the Lord as a thousand years, and a thousand years as one day.

The Lord is not slack concerning his promise, as some men count slackness; but is longsuffering to us-ward, not willing that any should perish, but that all should come to repentance.

But the day of the Lord will come as a thief in the night; in the which the heavens shall pass away with a great noise, and the elements shall melt with fervent heat, the earth also and the works that are therein shall be burned up.

Seeing then that all these things shall be dissolved, what manner of persons ought ye to be in all holy conversation and godliness,

Looking for and hasting unto the coming of the day of God, wherein the heavens being on fire shall be dissolved, and the elements shall melt with fervent heat?

Nevertheless we, according to this promise, look for new heavens and a new earth, wherein dwelleth righteousness.

II Peter 3:3, 4, 8-13

Beloved, now are we the sons of God, and it doth not yet appear what we shall be: but we know that, when he shall appear, we shall be like him; for we shall see him as he is.

And every man that hath this hope in him purifieth himself, even as he is pure.

I John 3:2,3

And there shall be signs in the sun, and in the moon, and in the stars; and upon the earth distress of nations, with perplexity; the sea and the waves roaring;

Men's hearts failing them for fear, and for looking after those things which are coming on the earth: for the powers of heaven shall be shaken.

And then shall they see the Son of man coming in a cloud with power and great glory.

And when these things begin to come to pass, then look up, and lift up your heads; for your redemption draweth nigh.

Luke 21:25-28

And as he sat upon the mount of Olives, the disciples came unto him privately, saying, Tell us, when shall these things be? and what shall be the sign of thy coming, and of the end of the world?

And Jesus answered and said unto them, Take heed that no man deceive you.

For many shall come in my name, saying, I am Christ; and shall deceive many.

And ye shall hear of wars and rumours of wars: see that ye be not troubled: for all these things must come to pass, but the end is not yet.

For nation shall rise against nation, and kingdom against kingdom: and there shall be famines, and pestilences, and earthquakes, in divers places.

All these are the beginning of sorrows.

Then shall they deliver you up to be afflicted, and shall kill you: and ye shall be hated of all nations for my name's sake.

And then shall many be offended, and shall betray one another, and shall hate one another.

And many false prophets shall rise, and shall deceive many.

And because iniquity shall abound, the love of many shall wax cold.

But he that shall endure unto the end, the same shall be saved.

And this gospel of the kingdom shall be preached in all the world for a witness unto all nations; and then shall the end come.

Matthew 24:3-14

For as the lightning cometh out of the east, and shineth even unto the west; so shall also the coming of the Son of man be.

Immediately after the tribulation of those days shall the sun be darkened, and the moon shall not give her light, and the stars shall fall from heaven, and the powers of the heavens shall be shaken:

And then shall appear the sign of the Son of man in heaven: and then shall all the tribes of the earth mourn, and they shall see the Son of man coming in the clouds of heaven with power and great glory.

And he shall send his angels with a great sound of a trumpet, and they shall gather together his elect from the four winds, from one end of the heaven to the other.

Matthew 24:27, 29-31

But of that day and hour knoweth no man, no, not the angels of heaven, but my Father only.

But as the days of Noe were, so shall also the coming of the Son of man be.

For as in the days that were before the flood they were eating and drinking, marrying and giving in marriage, until the day that Noe entered into the ark,

And knew not until the flood came, and took them all away; so shall also the coming of the Son of man be.

Then shall two be in the field; the one shall be taken, and the other left.

Two women shall be grinding at the mill; the one shall be taken, and the other left.

Watch therefore: for ye know not what hour your Lord doth come.

But know this, that if the goodman of the house had known in what watch the thief would come, he would have watched, and would not have suffered his house to be broken up.

Therefore be ye also ready: for in such an hour as ye think not the Son of man cometh.

Matthew 24:36-44

This know also, that in the last days perilous times shall come.

For men shall be lovers of their own selves, covetous, boasters, proud, blasphemers, disobedient to parents, unthankful, unholy,

Without natural affection, trucebreakers, false accusers, incontinent, fierce, despisers of those that are good,

Traitors, heady, highminded, lovers of pleasures more than lovers of God;

Having a form of godliness, but denying the power thereof: from such turn away.

II Timothy 3:1-5

Now the Spirit speaketh expressly, that in the latter times some shall depart from the faith, giving heed to seducing spirits, and doctrines of devils;

Speaking lies in hypocrisy; having their conscience seared with a hot iron;

Forbidding to marry, and commanding to abstain from meats, which God hath created to be received with thanksgiving of them which believe and know the truth.

I Timothy 4:1-3

I charge thee therefore before God, and the Lord Jesus Christ, who shall judge the quick and the dead at his appearing and his kingdom;

Preach the word; be instant in season, out of season; reprove, rebuke, exhort with all longsuffering and doctrine.

For the time will come when they will not endure sound doctrine; but after their own lusts shall they heap to themselves teachers, having itching ears;

And they shall turn away their ears from the truth, and shall be turned into fables.

But watch thou in all things, endure afflictions, do the work of an evangelist, make full proof of thy ministry.

For I am now ready to be offered, and the time of my departure is at hand.

I have fought a good fight, I have finished my course, I have kept the faith:

Henceforth there is laid up for me a crown of righteousness, which the Lord, the righteous judge, shall give me at that day: and not to me only, but unto all them also that love his appearing.

II Timothy 4:1-8

Verily I say unto you, This generation shall not pass, till all these things be fulfilled.

Matthew 24:34

Let not your heart be troubled: ye believe in God, believe also in me.

In my Father's house are many mansions: if it were not so, I would have told you. I go to prepare a place for you.

And if I go and prepare a place for you, I will come again, and receive you unto myself; that where I am, there ye may be also.

And whither I go ye know, and the way ye know.

John 14:1-4

The Unsaved

For all have sinned, and come short of the glory of God;

Romans 3:23

Wherefore, as by one man sin entered into the world, and death by sin; and so death passed upon all men, for that all have sinned:

Romans 5:12

For the wages of sin is death; but the gift of God is eternal life through Jesus Christ our Lord.

Romans 6:23

For the wrath of God is revealed from heaven against all ungodliness and unrighteousness of men, who hold the truth in unrighteousness;

Because that which may be known of God is manifest in them; for God hath shewed it unto them.

For the invisible things of him from the creation of the world are clearly seen, being understood by the things that are made, even his eternal power and Godhead; so that they are without excuse:

Romans 1:18-20

But God commendeth his love toward us, in that, while we were yet sinners, Christ died for us.

Romans 5:8

The Lord is not slack concerning his promise, as some men count slackness; but is longsuffering to us-ward, not willing that any should perish, but that all should come to repentance.

II Peter 3:9

For God sent not his Son into the world to condemn the world; but that the world through him might be saved.

John 3:17

I came not to call the righteous, but sinners to repentance.

Luke 5:32

For the Son of man is come to seek and to save that which was lost.

Luke 19:10

Jesus answered and said unto him, Verily, verily, I say unto thee, Except a man be born again, he cannot see the kingdom of God.

John 3:3

For God so loved the world, that he gave his only begotten Son, that whosoever believeth in him should not perish, but have everlasting life.

John 3:16

And they said, Believe on the Lord Jesus Christ, and thou shalt be saved, and thy house.

Acts 16:32

And he said unto them, Go ye into all the world, and preach the gospel to every creature.

He that believeth and is baptized shall be saved; but he that believeth not shall be damned.

Mark 16:15, 16

The Spirit of the Lord is upon me, because he hath anointed me to preach the gospel to the poor; he hath sent me to heal the brokenhearted, to preach deliverance to the captives, and recovering of sight to the blind, to set at liberty them that are bruised,

To preach the acceptable year of the Lord.

Luke 4:18, 19

Truth From The Bible About . . .

TRUTH FROM THE BIBLE ABOUT
Forgiving Others

For if ye forgive men their trespasses, your heavenly Father will also forgive you:

But if ye forgive not men their trespasses, neither will your Father forgive your trespasses.

Matthew 6:14, 15

Then came Peter to him, and said, Lord, how oft shall my brother sin against me, and I forgive him? till seven times?

Jesus saith unto him, I say not unto thee, Until seven times: but, Until seventy times seven.

Matthew 18:21, 22

Take heed to yourselves: If thy brother trespass against thee, rebuke him; and if he repent, forgive him.

Luke 17:3

And when ye stand praying, forgive, if ye have aught against any: that your Father also which is in heaven may forgive you your trespasses.

Mark 11:25

Forbearing one another, and forgiving one another, if any man have a quarrel against any: even as Christ forgave you, so also do ye.

Colossians 3:13

Brethren, I count not myself to have apprehended: but this one thing I do, forgetting those things which are behind, and reaching forth unto those things which are before,

I press toward the mark for the prize of the high calling of God in Christ Jesus.

Philippians 3:13, 14

Remember ye not the former things, neither consider the things of old.

Behold, I will do a new thing; now it shall spring forth; shall ye not know it? I will even make a way in the wilderness, and rivers in the desert.

Isaiah 43:18, 19

For this is thankworthy, if a man for conscience toward God endure grief, suffering wrongfully.

For what glory is it, if, when ye be buffeted for your faults, ye shall take it patiently? but if, when ye do well, and suffer for it, ye take it patiently, this is acceptable with God.

For even hereunto were ye called: because Christ also suffered for us, leaving us an example, that ye should follow his steps:

Who did no sin, neither was guile found in his mouth:

Who, when he was reviled, reviled not again; when he suffered, he threatened not; but committed himself to him that judgeth righteously:

I Peter 2:19-23

Blessed are they which are persecuted for righteousness' sake: for theirs is the kingdom of heaven.

Blessed are ye, when men shall revile you, and persecute you, and shall say all manner of evil against you falsely, for my sake.

Rejoice, and be exceeding glad: for great is your reward in heaven: for so persecuted they the prophets which were before you.

Matthew 5:10-12

For we know him that hath said, Vengeance belongeth unto me, I will recompense, saith the Lord. And again, The Lord shall judge his people.

Hebrews 10:30

Beloved, think it not strange concerning the fiery trial which is to try you, as though some strange thing happened unto you:

But rejoice, inasmuch as ye are partakers of Christ's sufferings; that, when his glory shall be revealed, ye may be glad also with exceeding joy.

If ye be reproached for the name of Christ, happy are ye; for the spirit of glory and of God resteth upon you: on their part he is evil spoken of, but on your part he is glorified.

I Peter 4:12-14

But I say unto you, Love your enemies, bless them that curse you, do good to them that hate you, and pray for them which despitefully use you, and persecute you;

Matthew 5:44

Be not overcome of evil, but overcome evil with good.

Romans 12:21

Not rendering evil for evil, or railing for railing: but contrariwise blessing; knowing that ye are thereunto called, that ye should inherit a blessing.

For he that will love life, and see good days, let him refrain his tongue from evil, and his lips that they speak no guile:

I Peter 3:9, 10

Let all bitterness, and wrath, and anger, and clamour, and evil speaking, be put away from you, with all malice:

And be ye kind one to another, tenderhearted, forgiving one another, even as God for Christ's sake hath forgiven you.

Ephesians 4:31, 32

Christian Fellowship

That which we have seen and heard declare we unto you, that ye also may have fellowship with us: and truly our fellowship is with the Father, and with his Son Jesus Christ.

But if we walk in the light, as he is in the light, we have fellowship one with another, and the blood of Jesus Christ his Son cleanseth us from all sin.

I John 1:3, 7

And walk in love, as Christ also hath loved us, and hath given himself for us an offering and a sacrifice to God for a sweet-smelling savour.

Speaking to yourselves in psalms and hymns and spiritual songs, singing and making melody in your heart to the Lord;

For we are members of his body, of his flesh, and of his bones.

Ephesians 5:2, 19, 30

Let the word of Christ dwell in you richly in all wisdom; teaching and admonishing one another in psalms and hymns and spiritual songs, singing with grace in your hearts to the Lord.

Colossians 3:16

That their hearts might be comforted, being knit together in love, and unto all riches of the full assurance of understanding, to the acknowledgement of the mystery of God, and of the Father, and of Christ;

Colossians 2:2

Then they that feared the Lord spake often one to another: and the Lord hearkened, and heard it, and a book of remembrance was written before him for them that feared the Lord, and that thought upon his name.

Malachi 3:16

And, behold, two of them went that same day to a village called Emmaus, which was from Jerusalem about threescore furlongs.

And they talked together of all these things which had happened.

And it came to pass, that, while they communed together and reasoned, Jesus himself drew near, and went with them.

Luke 24:13-15

We took sweet counsel together, and walked unto the house of God in company.

Psalm 55:14

And now I am no more in the world, but these are in the world, and I come to thee. Holy Father, keep through thine own name those whom thou hast given me, that they may be one, as we are.

That they all may be one; as thou, Father, art in me, and I in thee, that they also may be one in us: that the world may believe that thou hast sent me.

And the glory thou gavest me I have given them; that they may be one, even as we are one:

I in them, and thou in me, that they may be made perfect in one; and that the world may know that thou hast sent me, and hast loved them, as thou hast loved me.

John 17:11, 21-23

And when the day of Pentecost was fully come, they were all with one accord in one place.

And they continued stedfastly in the apostles' doctrine and fellowship, and in breaking of bread, and in prayers.

And they, continuing daily with one accord in the temple, and breaking bread from house to house, did eat their meat with gladness and singleness of heart,

Praising God, and having favour with all the people. And the Lord added to the church daily such as should be saved.

Acts 2:1, 42, 46, 47

Now the God of patience and consolation grant you to be likeminded one toward another according to Christ Jesus:

That ye may with one mind and one mouth glorify God, even the Father of our Lord Jesus Christ.

Wherefore receive ye one another, as Christ also received us to the glory of God.

Romans 15:5-7

Now I beseech you, brethren, by the name of our Lord Jesus Christ, that ye all speak the same thing, and that there be no divisions among you; but that ye be perfectly joined together in the same mind and in the same judgment.

I Corinthians 1:10

Bear ye one another's burdens, and so fulfil the law of Christ.

As we have therefore opportunity, let us do good unto all men, especially unto them who are of the household of faith.

Galatians 6:2, 10

Now therefore ye are no more strangers and foreigners, but fellow-citizens with the saints, and of the household of God;

And are built upon the foundation of the apostles and prophets, Jesus Christ himself being the chief corner stone;

In whom all the building fitly framed together groweth unto an holy temple in the Lord:

In whom ye also are builded together for an habitation of God through the Spirit.

Ephesians 2:19-22

I thank my God upon every remembrance of you,

Only let your conversation be as it becometh the gospel of Christ: that whether I come and see you, or else be absent, I may hear of your affairs, that ye stand fast in one spirit, with one mind striving together for the faith of the gospel;

Philippians 1:3, 27

If there be therefore any consolation in Christ, if any comfort of love, if any fellowship of the Spirit, if any bowels and mercies,

Fulfil ye my joy, that ye be likeminded, having the same love, being of one accord, of one mind.

Philippians 2:1, 2

And let us consider one another to provoke unto love and to good works·

Not forsaking the assembling of ourselves together, as the manner of some is; but exhorting one another: and so much the more, as ye see the day approaching.

Hebrews 10:24, 25

TRUTH FROM THE BIBLE ABOUT
Your Responsibility

And he said unto them, Go ye into all the world, and preach the gospel to every creature.

Mark 16:15

But ye shall receive power, after that the Holy Ghost is come upon you: and ye shall be witnesses unto me both in Jerusalem, and in all Judaea, and in Samaria, and unto the uttermost part of the earth.

Acts 1:8

Ye are the salt of the earth: but if the salt have lost his savour, wherewith shall it be salted? It is thenceforth good for nothing, but to be cast out, and to be trodden under foot of men.

Ye are the light of the world. A city that is set on an hill cannot be hid.

Neither do men light a candle, and put it under a bushel, but on a candlestick; and it giveth light unto all that are in the house.

Let your light so shine before men, that they may see your good works, and glorify your Father which is in heaven.

Matthew 5:13-16

For I was an hungered, and ye gave me meat: I was thirsty, and ye gave me drink: I was a stranger, and ye took me in:

Naked, and ye clothed me: I was sick, and ye visited me: I was in prison, and ye came unto me.

Then shall the righteous answer him, saying, Lord, when saw we thee an hungered, and fed thee? or thirsty, and gave thee drink?

When saw we thee a stranger, and took thee in? or naked, and clothed thee?

Or when saw we thee sick, or in prison, and came unto thee?

And the King shall answer and say unto them, Verily I say unto you, Inasmuch as ye have done it unto one of the least of these my brethren, ye have done it unto me.

Matthew 25:35-40

And whosoever shall give to drink unto one of these little ones a cup of cold water only in the name of a disciple, verily I say unto you, he shall in no wise lose his reward.

Matthew 10:42

For God is not unrighteous to forget your work and labour of love, which ye have shewed toward his name, in that ye have ministered to the saints, and do minister.

Hebrews 6:10

Pure religion and undefiled before God and the Father is this, To visit the fatherless and widows in their affliction, and to keep himself unspotted from the world.

James 1:27

If a brother or sister be naked, and destitute of daily food,

And one of you say unto them, Depart in peace, be ye warmed and filled; notwithstanding ye give them not those things which are needful to the body; what doth it profit?

Even so faith, if it hath not works, is dead, being alone.

James 2:15-17

And the people asked him, saying, What shall we do then?

He answereth and saith unto them, He that hath two coats, let him impart to him that hath none; and he that hath meat, let him do likewise.

Luke 3:10, 11

Brethren, if a man be overtaken in a fault, ye which are spiritual, restore such an one in the spirit of meekness; considering thyself, lest thou also be tempted.

Bear ye one another's burdens, and so fulfil the law of Christ.

For if a man think himself to be something, when he is nothing, he deceiveth himself.

But let every man prove his own work, and then shall he have rejoicing in himself alone, and not in another.

For every man shall bear his own burden.

Let him that is taught in the word communicate unto him that teacheth in all good things.

Galatians 6:1-6

Hereby perceive we the love of God, because he laid down his life for us: and we ought to lay down our lives for the brethren.

But whoso hath this world's good, and seeth his brother have need, and shutteth up his bowels of compassion from him, how dwelleth the love of God in him?

My little children, let us not love in word, neither in tongue; but in deed and in truth.

I John 3:16-18

And these words, which I command thee this day, shall be in thine heart:

And thou shalt teach them diligently unto thy children, and shalt talk of them when thou sittest in thine house, and when thou walkest by the way, and when thou liest down, and then when thou risest up.

And thou shalt bind them for a sign upon thine hand, and they shall be as frontlets between thine eyes.

And thou shalt write them upon the posts of thy house, and on thy gates.

Deuteronomy 6:6-9

But if any provide not for his own, and specially for those of his own house, he hath denied the faith, and is worse than an infidel.

I Timothy 5:8

Train up a child in the way he should go: and when he is old, he will not depart from it.

Proverbs 22:6

Therefore shall ye lay up these my words in your heart and in your soul, and bind them for a sign upon your hand, that they may be as frontlets between your eyes.

And ye shall teach them your children, speaking of them when thou sittest in thine house, and when thou walkest by the way, when thou liest down, and when thou risest up.

Deuteronomy 11:18, 19

Speaking God's Word

For verily I say unto you, That whosoever shall say unto this mountain, Be thou removed, and be thou cast into the sea; and shall not doubt in his heart, but shall believe that those things which he saith shall come to pass; he shall have whatsoever he saith.

Mark 11:23

And the Lord said, If ye had faith as a grain of mustard seed, ye might say unto this sycamine tree, Be thou plucked up by the root, and be thou planted in the sea; and it should obey you.

Luke 17:6

And he arose, and rebuked the wind, and said unto the sea, Peace, be still. And the wind ceased, and there was a great calm.

Mark 4:39

Through faith we understand that the worlds were framed by the word of God, so that things which are seen were not made of things which do appear.

Hebrews 11:3

For I have not spoken of myself; but the Father which sent me, he gave me a commandment, what I should say, and what I should speak.

And I know that his commandment is life everlasting; whatsoever I speak therefore, even as the Father said unto me, so I speak.

John 12: 49, 50

I will raise them up a Prophet from among their brethren, like unto thee, and will put my words in his mouth; and he shall speak unto them all that I shall command him.

Deuteronomy 18:18

Bless the Lord, ye his angels, that excel in strength, that do his commandments, hearkening unto the voice of his word.

Psalm 103:20

The wise in heart shall be called prudent: and the sweetness of the lips increaseth learning.

The heart of the wise teacheth his mouth, and addeth learning to his lips.

Pleasant words are as an honeycomb, sweet to the soul, and health to the bones.

An ungodly man diggeth up evil: and in his lips there is as a burning fire.

He shutteth his eyes to devise froward things: moving his lips he bringeth evil to pass.

Proverbs 16:21, 23, 24, 27, 30

The words of a man's mouth are as deep waters, and the wellspring of wisdom as a flowing brook.

A fool's mouth is his destruction, and his lips are the snare of his soul.

A man's belly shall be satisfied with the fruit of his mouth; and with the increase of his lips shall he be filled.

Death and life are in the power of the tongue: and they that love it shall eat the fruit thereof.

Proverbs 18:4, 7, 20, 21

...for out of the abundance of the heart the mouth speaketh.

But I say unto you, That every idle word that men shall speak, they shall give account thereof in the day of judgment.

For by thy words thou shalt be justified, and by thy words thou shalt be condemned.

Matthew 12: 34b, 36, 37

If any man among you seem to be religious, and bridleth not his tongue, but deceiveth his own heart, this man's religion is vain.

James 1:26

But the righteousness which is of faith speaketh on this wise,

But what saith it? The word is nigh thee, even in thy mouth, and in thy heart: that is, the word of faith, which we preach;

That if thou shalt confess with thy mouth the Lord Jesus, and shalt believe in thine heart that God hath raised him from the dead, thou shalt be saved.

For with the heart man believeth unto righteousness; and with the mouth confession is made unto salvation.

Romans 10: 6a, 8-10

Let us hold fast the profession of our faith without wavering; (for he is faithful that promised;)

Hebrews 10:23

We having the same spirit of faith, according as it is written, I believed, and therefore have I spoken; we also believe, and therefore speak;

II Corinthians 4:13

Beat your plowshares into swords, and your pruninghooks into spears: let the weak say, I am strong.

Joel 3:10

A man shall eat good by the fruit of his mouth: but the soul of the transgressors shall eat violence.

He that keepeth his mouth keepeth his life: but he that openeth wide his lips shall have destruction.

Proverbs 13:2, 3

There is that speaketh like the piercings of a sword: but the tongue of the wise is health.

Proverbs 12:18

Finding The Will Of God

If any of you lack wisdom, let him ask of God, that giveth to all men liberally, and upbraideth not; and it shall be given him.

James 1:5

I will instruct thee and teach thee in the way which thou shalt go: I will guide thee with mine eye.

Psalm 32:8

Thy word is a lamp unto my feet, and a light unto my path.

Psalm 119:105

When thou goest, it shall lead thee; when thou sleepest, it shall keep thee; and when thou awakest, it shall talk with thee.

For the commandment is a lamp; and the law is light; and reproofs of instruction are the way of life:

Proverbs 6:22, 23

This book of the law shall not depart out of thy mouth; but thou shalt meditate therein day and night, that thou mayest observe to do according to all that is written therein: for then thou shalt make thy way prosperous, and then thou shalt have good success.

Joshua 1:8

And thine ears shall hear a word behind thee, saying, This is the way, walk ye in it, when ye turn to the right hand, and when ye turn to the left.

Isaiah 30:21

For this God is our God for ever and ever: he will be our guide even unto death.

Psalm 48:14

Commit thy works unto the Lord, and thy thoughts shall be established.

Proverbs 16:3

The steps of a good man are ordered by the Lord; and he delighteth in his way.

Psalm 37:23

For thou art my rock and my fortress; therefore for thy name's sake lead me, and guide me.

Psalm 31:3

Thou gavest also thy good spirit to instruct them, and withheldest not thy manna from their mouth, and gavest them water for their thirst.

Nehemiah 9:20

Trust in the Lord with all thine heart; and lean not unto thine own understanding.
In all thy ways acknowledge him, and he shall direct thy paths.

Proverbs 3:5, 6

Thus saith the Lord, thy Redeemer, the Holy One of Israel; I am the Lord thy God which teacheth thee to profit, which leadeth thee by the way that thou shouldest go.

Isaiah 48:17

And the Lord shall guide thee continually, and satisfy thy soul in drought, and make fat thy bones: and thou shalt be like a watered garden, and like a spring of water, whose waters fail not.

Isaiah 58:11

Howbeit when he, the Spirit of truth, is come, he will guide you into all truth: for he shall not speak of himself; but whatsoever he shall hear, that shall he speak: and he will shew you things to come.

John 16:13

Answered Prayer

And it shall come to pass, that before they call, I will answer; and while they are yet speaking, I will hear.

Isaiah 65:24

Ask, and it shall be given you; seek, and ye shall find; knock, and it shall be opened unto you:

For every one that asketh receiveth; and he that seeketh findeth, and to him that knocketh it shall be opened.

Matthew 7:7, 8

And all things, whatsoever ye shall ask in prayer, believing, ye shall receive.

Matthew 21:22

Again I say unto you, That if two of you shall agree on earth as touching any thing that they shall ask, it shall be done for them of my Father which is in heaven.

For where two or three are gathered together in my name, there am I in the midst of them.

Matthew 18:19, 20

Therefore I say unto you, What things soever ye desire, when ye pray, believe that ye receive them, and ye shall have them.

Mark 11:24

And whatsoever ye shall ask in my name, that will I do, that the Father may be glorified in the Son.

John 14:13

If ye abide in me, and my words abide in you, ye shall ask what ye will, and it shall be done unto you.

John 15:7

And in that day ye shall ask me nothing. Verily, verily, I say unto you, Whatsoever ye shall ask the Father in my name, he will give it you.

John 16:23

Let us therefore come boldly unto the throne of grace, that we may obtain mercy, and find grace to help in time of need.

Hebrews 4:16

Delight thyself also in the Lord; and he shall give thee the desires of thine heart.

Psalm 37:4

He shall call upon me, and I will answer him: I will be with him in trouble; I will deliver him, and honour him.

Psalm 91:15

The Lord is nigh unto all them that call upon him, to all that call upon him in truth.

He will fulfil the desire of them that fear him: he also will hear their cry, and will save them.

Psalm 145:18, 19

The Lord is far from the wicked: but he heareth the prayer of the righteous.

Proverbs 15:29

Call unto me, and I will answer thee, and shew thee great and mighty things, which thou knowest not.

Jeremiah 33:3

But thou, when thou prayest, enter into thy closet, and when thou hast shut thy door, pray to thy Father which is in secret; and thy Father which seeth in secret shall reward thee openly.

Matthew 6:6

And whatsoever we ask, we receive of him, because we keep his commandments, and do those things that are pleasing in his sight.

I John 3:22

Unsaved Loved Ones

And they said, Believe on the Lord Jesus Christ, and thou shalt be saved, and thy house.

Acts 16:31

Who shall tell thee words, whereby thou and all thy house shall be saved.

Acts 11:14

Even so it is not the will of your Father which is in heaven, that one of these little ones should perish.

Matthew 18:14

For I will pour water upon him that is thirsty, and floods upon the dry ground: I will pour my spirit upon thy seed, and my blessing upon thine offspring:

Isaiah 44:3

The Lord is not slack concerning his promise, as some men count slackness; but is longsuffering to us-ward, not willing that any should perish, but that all should come to repentance.

II Peter 3:9

Likewise, ye wives, be in subjection to your own husbands; that, if any obey not the word, they also may without the word be won by the conversation of the wives;

While they behold your chaste conversation coupled with fear.

I Peter 3:1, 2

And the woman which hath a husband that believeth not, and if he be pleased to dwell with her, let her not leave him.

For the unbelieving husband is sanctified by the wife, and the unbelieving wife is sanctified by the husband: else were your children unclean; but now are they holy.

But if the unbelieving depart, let him depart. A brother or a sister is not under bondage in such cases: but God hath called us to peace.

For what knowest thou, O wife, whether thou shalt save thy husband? or how knowest thou, O man, whether thou shalt save thy wife?

I Corinthians 7:13-16

Prove all things; hold fast that which is good.

Abstain from all appearance of evil.

I Thessalonians 5:21, 22

The Lord hath made known his salvation: his righteousness hath he openly shewed in the sight of the heathen.

Psalm 98:2

Who is among you that feareth the Lord, that obeyeth the voice of his servant, that walketh in darkness, and hath no light? let him trust in the name of the Lord, and stay upon his God.

Isaiah 50:10

Cast thy burden upon the Lord, and he shall sustain thee: he shall never suffer the righteous to be moved.

Psalm 55:22

Thus saith the Lord, Keep ye judgment, and do justice: for my salvation is near to come, and my righteousness to be revealed.

Isaiah 56:1

Nevertheless I tell you the truth; It is expedient for you that I go away: for if I go not away, the Comforter will not come unto you; but if I depart, I will send him unto you.

And when he is come, he will reprove the world of sin, and of righteousness, and of judgment:

John 16:7, 8

Train up a child in the way he should go: and when he is old, he will not depart from it.

Proverbs 22:6

Faithful is he that calleth you, who also will do it.

I Thessalonians 5:24

Marriage

And the Lord God said, It is not good that the man should be alone; I will make him an help meet for him.

Genesis 2:18

Therefore shall a man leave his father and his mother, and shall cleave unto his wife: and they shall be one flesh.

Genesis 2:24

Whoso findeth a wife findeth a good thing, and obtaineth favour of the Lord.

Proverbs 18:22

Take ye wives, and beget sons and daughters; and take wives for your sons, and give your daughters to husbands, that they may bear sons and daughters; that ye may be increased there, and not diminished.

Jeremiah 29:6

And I will betroth thee unto me for ever; yea, I will betroth thee unto me in righteousness, and in judgment, and in loving kindness, and in mercies.

I will even betroth thee unto me in faithfulness: and thou shalt know the Lord.

Hosea 2:19, 20

Nevertheless, to avoid fornication, let every man have his own wife, and let every woman have her own husband.

Let the husband render unto the wife due benevolence: and likewise also the wife unto the husband.

The wife hath not power of her own body, but the husband; and likewise also the husband hath not power of his own body, but the wife.

I Corinthians 7:2-4

I will therefore that the younger women marry, bear children, guide the house, give none occasion to the adversary to speak reproachfully.

I Timothy 5:14

Marriage is honourable in all, and the bed undefiled: but whoremongers and adulterers God will judge.

Hebrews 13:4

Wives, submit yourselves unto your own husbands, as unto the Lord.

For the husband is the head of the wife, even as Christ is the head of the church: and he is the saviour of the body.

Therefore as the church is subject unto Christ, so let the wives be to their own husbands in every thing.

Husbands, love your wives, even as Christ also loved the church, and gave himself for it;

That he might sanctify and cleanse it with the washing of water by the word,

That he might present it to himself a glorious church, not having spot, or wrinkle, or any such thing; but that it should be holy and without blemish.

So ought men to love their wives as their own bodies. He that loveth his wife loveth himself.

For no man ever yet hated his own flesh; but nourisheth and cherisheth it, even as the Lord the church:

For we are members of his body, of his flesh, and of his bones.

For this cause shall a man leave his father and mother, and shall be joined unto his wife, and they two shall be one flesh.

This is a great mystery: but I speak concerning Christ and the church.

Nevertheless let every one of you in particular so love his wife even as himself; and the wife see that she reverence her husband.

Ephesians 5:22-33

Likewise, ye wives, be in subjection to your own husbands; that, if any obey not the word, they also may without the word be won by the conversation of the wives.

I Peter 3:1

Likewise, ye husbands, dwell with them according to knowledge, giving honour unto the wife, as unto the weaker vessel, and as being heirs together of the grace of life; that your prayers be not hindered.

I Peter 3:7

Divorce

It hath been said, Whosoever shall put away his wife, let him give her a writing of divorcement:

But I say unto you, That whosoever shall put away his wife, saving for the cause of fornication, causeth her to commit adultery: and whosoever shall marry her that is divorced committeth adultery.

Matthew 5:31, 32

The Pharisees also came unto him, tempting him, and saying unto him, Is it lawful for a man to put away his wife for every cause?

And he answered and said unto them, Have ye not read, that he which made them at the beginning made them male and female,

And said, For this cause shall a man leave father and mother, and shall cleave to his wife: and they twain shall be one flesh?

Wherefore they are no more twain, but one flesh. What therefore God hath joined together, let not man put asunder.

They say unto him, Why did Moses then command to give a writing of divorcement, and put her away?

He saith unto them, Moses because of the hardness of your hearts suffered you to put away your wives: but from the beginning it was not so.

And I say unto you, Whosoever shall put away his wife, except it be for fornication, and shall marry another, committeth adultery: and whoso marrieth her which is put away doth commit adultery.

Matthew 19:3-9

And the Pharisees came to him, and asked him, Is it lawful for a man to put away his wife? tempting him.

And he answered and said unto them, What did Moses command you?

And they said, Moses suffered to write a bill of divorcement, and to put her away.

And Jesus answered and said unto them, For the hardness of your heart he wrote you this precept.

But from the beginning of the creation God made them male and female.

For this cause shall a man leave his father and mother, and cleave to his wife;

And they twain shall be one flesh: so then they are no more twain, but one flesh.

What therefore God hath joined together, let not man put asunder.

And in the house his disciples asked him again of the same matter.

And he saith unto them, Whosoever shall put away his wife, and marry another, committeth adultery against her.

And if a woman shall put away her husband, and be married to another, she committeth adultery.

Mark 10:2-12

Whosoever putteth away his wife, and marrieth another, committeth adultery: and whosoever marrieth her that is put away from her husband committeth adultery.

Luke 16:18

And unto the married I command, yet not I, but the Lord, Let not the wife depart from her husband:

But and if she depart, let her remain unmarried, or be reconciled to her husband: and let not the husband put away his wife.

But to the rest speak I, not the Lord: If any brother hath a wife that believeth not, and she be pleased to dwell with him, let him not put her away.

And the woman which hath an husband that believeth not, and if he be pleased to dwell with her, let her not leave him.

For the unbelieving husband is sanctified by the wife, and the unbelieving wife is sanctified by the husband: else were your children unclean; but now are they holy.

But if the unbelieving depart, let him depart. A brother or a sister is not under bondage in such cases: but God hath called us to peace.

For what knowest thou, O wife, whether thou shalt save thy husband? or how knowest thou, O man, whether thou shalt save thy wife?

But as God hath distributed to every man, as the Lord hath called every one, so let him walk. And so ordain I in all churches.

I Corinthians 7:10-17

When a man hath taken a wife, and married her, and it come to pass that she find no favour in his eyes, because he hath found some uncleanness in her: then let him write her a bill of divorcement, and give it in her hand, and send her out of his house.

And when she is departed out of his house, she may go and be another man's wife.

And if the latter husband hate her, and write her a bill of divorcement, and giveth it in her hand, and sendeth her out of his house; or if the latter husband die, which took her to be his wife;

Her former husband, which sent her away, may not take her again to be his wife, after that she is defiled; for that is abomination before the Lord: and thou shalt not cause the land to sin, which the Lord thy God giveth thee for an inheritance.

Deuteronomy 24:1-4

They say, If a man put away his wife, and she go from him, and become another man's, shall he return unto her again? shall not that land be greatly polluted? but thou hast played the harlot with many lovers; yet return again to me, saith the Lord.

Jeremiah 3:1

Your Family

And they said, Believe on the Lord Jesus Christ, and thou shalt be saved, and thy house.

Acts 16:31

And if it seem evil unto you to serve the Lord, choose you this day whom ye will serve; whether the gods which your fathers served that were on the other side of the flood, or the gods of the Amorites, in whose land ye dwell: but as for me and my house, we will serve the Lord.

Joshua 24:15

Let all bitterness, and wrath, and anger, and clamour, and evil speaking, be put away from you, with all malice:

And be ye kind one to another, tender-hearted, forgiving one another, even as God for Christ's sake hath forgiven you.

Ephesians 4:31, 32

Train up a child in the way he should go: and when he is old, he will not depart from it.

Proverbs 22:6

Honour thy father and thy mother: that thy days may be long upon the land which the Lord thy God giveth thee.

Exodus 20:12

Submitting yourselves one to another in the fear of God.

Wives, submit yourselves unto your own husbands, as unto the Lord.

For the husband is the head of the wife, even as Christ is the head of the church: and he is the saviour of the body.

Therefore as the church is subject unto Christ, so let the wives be to their own husbands in every thing.

Husbands, love your wives, even as Christ also loved the church, and gave himself for it;

That he might sanctify and cleanse it with the washing of water by the word,

That he might present it to himself a glorious church, not having spot, or wrinkle, or any such thing; but that it should be holy and without blemish.

So ought men to love their wives as their own bodies. He that loveth his wife loveth himself.

For no man ever yet hated his own flesh; but nourisheth and cherisheth it, even as the Lord the church:

For we are members of his body, of his flesh, and of his bones.

For this cause shall a man leave his father and mother, and shall be joined unto his wife, and they two shall be one flesh.

This is a great mystery: but I speak concerning Christ and the church.

Nevertheless let every one of you in particular so love his wife even as himself; and the wife see that she reverence her husband.

Children, obey your parents in the Lord: for this is right.

Honour thy father and mother; which is the first commandment with promise;

That it may be well with thee, and thou mayest live long on the earth.

And, ye fathers, provoke not your children to wrath: but bring them up in the nurture and admonition of the Lord.

Ephesians 5:21-6:4

One that ruleth well his own house, having his children in subjection with all gravity;

(For if a man know not how to rule his own house, how shall he take care of the church of God?)

I Timothy 3:4, 5

Lo, children are an heritage of the Lord: and the fruit of the womb is his reward.

As arrows are in the hand of a mighty man; so are children of the youth.

Happy is the man that hath his quiver full of them: they shall not be ashamed, but they shall speak with the enemies in the gate.

Psalms 127:3-5

And he shall turn the heart of the fathers to the children, and the heart of the children to their fathers, lest I come and smite the earth with a curse.

Malachi 4:6

Children's children are the crown of old men; and the glory of children are their fathers.

Proverbs 17:6

And these words, which I command thee this day, shall be in thine heart:

And thou shalt teach them diligently unto thy children, and shalt talk of them when thou sittest in thine house, and when thou walkest by the way, and when thou liest down, and when thou risest up.

And thou shalt bind them for a sign upon thine hand, and they shall be as frontlets between thine eyes.

And thou shalt write them upon the posts of thy house, and on thy gates.

Deuteronomy 6:6-9

Correct thy son, and he shall give thee rest; yea, he shall give delight unto thy soul.

Proverbs 29:17

And, ye fathers, provoke not your children to wrath: but bring them up in the nurture and admonition of the Lord.

Ephesians 6:4

A good man leaveth an inheritance to his children's children: and the wealth of the sinner is laid up for the just.

Proverbs 13:22

Blessed is every one that feareth the Lord; that walketh in his ways.

For thou shalt eat the labour of thine hands: happy shalt thou be, and it shall be well with thee.

Thy wife shall be as a fruitful vine by the sides of thine house: thy children like olive plants round about thy table.

Behold, that thus shall the man be blessed that feareth the Lord.

Psalms 128:1-4

The father of the righteous shall greatly rejoice: and he that begetteth a wise child shall have joy of him.

Proverbs 23:24

And all thy children shall be taught of the Lord; and great shall be the peace of thy children.

Isaiah 54:13

TRUTH FROM THE BIBLE ABOUT
Wives

Whoso findeth a wife findeth a good thing, and obtaineth favour of the Lord.
Proverbs 18:22

Likewise, ye wives, be in subjection to your own husbands; that, if any obey not the word, they also may without the word be won by the conversation of the wives;

While they behold your chaste conversation coupled with fear.

Whose adorning let it not be that outward adorning of plaiting the hair, and of wearing of gold, or of putting on of apparel;

But let it be the hidden man of the heart, in that which is not corruptible, even the ornament of a meek and quiet spirit, which is in the sight of God of great price.

For after this manner in the old time the holy women also, who trusted in God, adorned themselves, being in subjection unto their own husbands:

Even as Sara obeyed Abraham, calling him lord: whose daughters ye are, as long as ye do well, and are not afraid with any amazement.

Likewise, ye husbands, dwell with them according to knowledge, giving honour unto the wife, as unto the weaker vessel, and as being heirs together of the grace of life; that your prayers be not hindered.

I Peter 3:1-7

Live joyfully with the wife whom thou lovest all the days of the life of thy vanity, which he hath given thee under the sun, all the days of thy vanity: for that is thy portion in this life, and in thy labour which thou takest under the sun.

Ecclesiastes 9:9

Let the husband render unto the wife due benevolence: and likewise also the wife unto the husband.

I Corinthians 7:3

Let thy fountain be blessed: and rejoice with the wife of thy youth.
Let her be as the loving hind and pleasant roe; Let her breasts satisfy thee at all times; and be thou ravished always with her love.

Proverbs 5:18, 19

Wives, submit yourselves unto your own husbands, as it is fit in the Lord.

Colossians 3:18

Thy wife shall be as a fruitful vine by the sides of thine house: thy children like olive plants round about thy table.

Psalms 128:3

Submitting yourselves one to another in the fear of God.

Wives, submit yourselves unto your own husbands, as unto the Lord.

For the husband is the head of the wife, even as Christ is the head of the church: and he is the saviour of the body.

Therefore as the church is subject unto Christ, so let the wives be to their own husbands in every thing.

Husbands, love your wives, even as Christ also loved the church, and gave himself for it;

That he might sanctify and cleanse it with the washing of water by the word,

That he might present it to himself a glorious church, not having spot, or wrinkle, or any such thing; but that it should be holy and without blemish.

So ought men to love their wives as their own bodies. He that loveth his wife loveth himself.

For no man ever yet hated his own flesh; but nourisheth and cherisheth it, even as the Lord the church:

For we are members of his body, of his flesh, and of his bones.

For this cause shall a man leave his father and mother, and shall be joined unto his wife, and they two shall be one flesh.

This is a great mystery: but I speak concerning Christ and the church.

Nevertheless let every one of you in particular so love his wife even as himself; and the wife see that she reverence her husband.

Ephesians 5:21-33

Who can find a virtuous woman? for her price is far above rubies.

The heart of her husband doth safely trust in her, so that he shall have no need of spoil.

She will do him good and not evil all the days of her life.

She seeketh wool, and flax, and worketh willingly with her hands.

She is like the merchants ships; she bringeth her food from afar.

She riseth also while it is yet night, and giveth meat to her household, and a portion to her maidens.

She considereth a field, and buyeth it: with the fruit of her hands she planteth a vineyard.

She girdeth her loins with strength, and strengtheneth her arms.

She perceiveth that her merchandise is good: her candle goeth not out by night.

She layeth her hands to the spindle, and her hands hold the distaff.

She stretcheth out her hand to the poor; yea, she reacheth forth her hands to the needy.

She is not afraid of the snow for her household: for all her household are clothed with scarlet.

She maketh herself coverings of tapestry; her clothing is silk and purple.

Her husband is known in the gates, when he sitteth among the elders of the land.

She maketh fine linen, and selleth it; and delivereth girdles unto the merchant.

Strength and honour are her clothing; and she shall rejoice in time to come.

She openeth her mouth with wisdom; and in her tongue is the law of kindness.

She looketh well to the ways of her household, and eateth not the bread of idleness.

Her children arise up, and call her blessed; her husband also, and he praiseth her.

Many daughters have done virtuously, but thou excellest them all.

Favour is deceitful, and beauty is vain; but a woman that feareth the Lord, she shall be praised.

Give her of the fruit of her hands; and let her own works praise her in the gates.

Proverbs 31:10-31

A virtuous woman is a crown to her husband: but she that maketh ashamed is as rottenness in his bones.

Proverbs 12:4

Every wise woman buildeth her house: but the foolish plucketh it down with her hands.

Proverbs 14:1

House and riches are the inheritance of fathers: and a prudent wife is from the Lord.

Proverbs 19:14

Widows

Pure religion and undefiled before God and the Father is this, To visit the fatherless and widows in their affliction, and to keep himself unspotted from the world.

James 1:27

The blessing of him that was ready to perish came upon me: and I caused the widow's heart to sing for joy.

Job 29:13

He doth execute the judgment of the fatherless and widow, and loveth the stranger, in giving him food and raiment.

Deuteronomy 10:18

The Lord will destroy the house of the proud: but he will establish the border of the widow.

Proverbs 15:25

The Lord preserveth the strangers; he relieveth the fatherless and widow: but the way of the wicked he turneth upside down.

Psalms 146:9

Leave thy fatherless children, I will preserve them alive; and let thy widows trust in me.

Jeremiah 49:11

For thy Maker is thine husband; the Lord of hosts is his name; and thy Redeemer the Holy One of Israel; The God of the whole earth shall he be called.

Isaiah 54:5

The wife is bound by the law as long as her husband liveth; but if her husband be dead, she is at liberty to be married to whom she will; only in the Lord.

But she is happier if she so abide, after my judgment: and I think also that I have the Spirit of God.

I Corinthians 7:39, 40

I will not leave you comfortless: I will come to you.

John 14:18

He healeth the broken in heart, and bindeth up their wounds.

Psalm 147:3

A father of the fatherless, and a judge of the widows, is God in his holy habitation.

Psalm 68:5

Cursed be he that perverteth the judgment of the stranger, fatherless, and widow. And all the people shall say, Amen.

Deuteronomy 27:19

By him therefore let us offer the sacrifice of praise to God continually, that is, the fruit of our lips giving thanks to his name.

Hebrews 13:15

Teaching them to observe all things whatsoever I have commanded you: and, lo, I am with you alway, even unto the end of the world. Amen.

Matthew 28:20

And ye now therefore have sorrow: but I will see you again, and your heart shall rejoice, and your joy no man taketh from you.

John 16:22

TRUTH FROM THE BIBLE ABOUT
Singles

And I will betroth thee unto me for ever; yea, I will betroth thee unto me in righteousness, and in judgment, and in lovingkindness, and in mercies.

Hosea 2:19

I say therefore to the unmarried and widows, It is good for them if they abide even as I.

I Corinthians 7:8

But as God hath distributed to every man, as the Lord hath called every one, so let him walk. And so ordain I in all churches.

I Corinthians 7:17

Art thou bound unto a wife? seek not to be loosed. Art thou loosed from a wife? seek not a wife.

But and if thou marry, thou hast not sinned; and if a virgin marry she hath not sinned. Nevertheless such shall have trouble in the flesh: but I spare you.

I Corinthians 7:27, 28

But I would have you without carefulness. He that is unmarried careth for the things that belong to the Lord, how he may please the Lord:

But he that is married careth for the things that are of the world, how he may please his wife.

And this I speak for your own profit; not that I may cast a snare upon you, but for that which is comely, and that ye may attend upon the Lord without distraction.

I Corinthians 7:32, 33, 35

Nevertheless he that standeth stedfast in his heart, having no necessity, but hath power over his own will, and hath so decreed in his heart that he will keep his virgin, doeth well.

I Corinthians 7:37

Marriage is honourable in all, and the bed undefiled: but whoremongers and adulterers God will judge.

Hebrews 13:4

Trust in the Lord with all thine heart; and lean not unto thine own understanding.

In all thy ways acknowledge him, and he shall direct thy paths.

Proverbs 3:5, 6

Delight thyself also in the Lord; and he shall give thee the desires of thine heart.

Psalm 37:4

Wherefore, my brethren, ye also are become dead to the law by the body of Christ; that ye should be married to another, even to him who is raised from the dead, that we should bring forth fruit unto God.

Romans 7:4

But let every man prove his own work, and then shall he have rejoicing in himself alone, and not in another.

Galatians 6:4

And to knowledge temperance; and to temperance patience; and to patience godliness;

And to godliness brotherly kindness; and to brotherly kindness charity.

For if these things be in you, and abound, they make you that ye shall neither be barren nor unfruitful in the knowledge of our Lord Jesus Christ.

II Peter 1:6-8

The Elderly

And even to your old age I am he; and even to hoar hairs will I carry you: I have made, and I will bear; even I will carry, and will deliver you.

Isaiah 46:4

O God, thou hast taught me from my youth: and hitherto have I declared thy wondrous works.

Now also when I am old and greyheaded, O God, forsake me not; until I have shewed thy strength unto this generation, and thy power to every one that is to come.

Psalm 71:17, 18

The glory of young men is their strength: and the beauty of old men is the grey head.

Proverbs 20:29

The hoary head is a crown of glory, if it be found in the way of righteousness.

Proverbs 16:31

They shall still bring forth fruit in old age; they shall be fat and flourishing;

Psalm 92:14

For length of days, and long life, and peace, shall they add to thee.

Proverbs 3:2

With long life will I satisfy him, and shew him my salvation.

Psalm 91:16

I have been young, and now am old; yet have I not seen the righteous forsaken, nor his seed begging bread.

Psalm 37:25

Let your conversation be without covetousness; and be content with such things as ye have: for he hath said, I will never leave thee, nor forsake thee.

Hebrews 13:5

For what is our hope, or joy, or crown of rejoicing? Are not even ye in the presence of our Lord Jesus Christ at his coming?

I Thessalonians 2:19

Yea though I walk through the valley of the shadow of death, I will fear no evil: for thou art with me; thy rod and thy staff they comfort me.

Psalm 23:4

When the poor and needy seek water, and there is none, and their tongue faileth for thirst, I the Lord will hear them, I the God of Israel will not forsake them.

Isaiah 41:17

Because thou shalt forget thy misery,
and remember it as waters that pass away:

Job 11:16

Why art thou cast down, O my soul?
and why art thou disquieted in me? hope
thou in God: for I shall yet praise him for the
help of his countenance.

Psalm 42:5

For I am persuaded, that neither
death, nor life, nor angels, nor principalities,
nor powers, nor things present, nor things to
come,

Nor height, nor depth, nor any other
creature, shall be able to separate us from
the love of God, which is in Christ Jesus our
Lord.

Romans 8:38, 39

For since the beginning of the world
men have not heard, nor perceived by the
ear, neither hath the eye seen, O God, beside
thee, what he hath prepared for him that
waiteth for him.

Isaiah 64:4

Surely goodness and mercy shall follow
me all the days of my life: and I will dwell in
the house of the Lord for ever.

Psalm 23:6

What You Can Do To . . .

WHAT YOU CAN DO TO
Grow Spiritually

But grow in grace, and in the knowledge of our Lord and Saviour Jesus Christ. To him be glory both now and for ever. Amen.

II Peter 3:18

As newborn babes, desire the sincere milk of the word, that ye may grow thereby:
If so be ye have tasted that the Lord is gracious.

I Peter 2:2, 3

Study to shew thyself approved unto God, a workman that needeth not to be ashamed, rightly dividing the word of truth.

II Timothy 2:15

Meditate upon these things; give thyself wholly to them; that thy profiting may appear to all.

I Timothy 4:15

Therefore leaving the principles of the doctrine of Christ, let us go on unto perfection;

Hebrews 6:1a

And beside this, giving all diligence, add to your faith virtue; and to virtue knowledge;

And to knowledge temperance; and to temperance patience; and to patience godliness;

And to godliness brotherly kindness; and to brotherly kindness charity.

For if these things be in you, and abound, they make you that ye shall neither be barren nor unfruitful in the knowledge of our Lord Jesus Christ.

II Peter 1:5-8

For this cause I bow my knees unto the Father of our Lord Jesus Christ,

Of whom the whole family in heaven and earth is named,

That he would grant you, according to the riches of his glory, to be strengthened with might by his Spirit in the inner man;

That Christ may dwell in your hearts by faith; that ye, being rooted and grounded in love,

May be able to comprehend with all saints what is the breadth, and length, and depth, and height;

And to know the love of Christ, which passeth knowledge, that ye might be filled with all the fulness of God.

Ephesians 3:14-19

For this cause we also, since the day we heard it, do not cease to pray for you, and to desire that ye might be filled with the knowledge of his will in all wisdom and spiritual understanding;

That ye might walk worthy of the Lord unto all pleasing, being fruitful in every good work, and increasing in the knowledge of God;

Strengthened with all might, according to his glorious power, unto all patience and longsuffering with joyfulness;

Colossians 1:9-11

Let the word of Christ dwell in you richly in all wisdom; teaching and admonishing one another in psalms and hymns and spiritual songs, singing with grace in your hearts to the Lord.

Colossians 3:16

But we all, with open face beholding as in a glass the glory of the Lord, are changed into the same image from glory to glory, even as by the Spirit of the Lord.

II Corinthians 3:18

The righteous shall flourish like the palm tree: he shall grow like a cedar in Lebanon.

Psalm 92:12

Being confident of this very thing, that he which hath begun a good work in you will perform it until the day of Jesus Christ:

And this I pray, that your love may abound yet more and more in knowledge and in all judgment;

That ye may approve things that are excellent; that ye may be sincere and without offence till the day of Christ;

Philippians 1:6, 9, 10

That we henceforth be no more children, tossed to and fro, and carried about with every wind of doctrine, by the sleight of men, and cunning craftiness, whereby they lie in wait to deceive;

But speaking the truth in love, may grow up into him in all things, which is the head, even Christ:

Ephesians 4:14, 15

Change The World

Ye are the light of the world. A city that is set on an hill cannot be hid.

Neither do men light a candle, and put it under a bushel, but on a candlestick; and it giveth light unto all that are in the house.

Let your light so shine before men, that they may see your good works, and glorify your Father which is in heaven.

Matthew 5:14-16

And they that be wise shall shine as the brightness of the firmament; and they that turn many to righteousness as the stars for ever and ever.

Daniel 12:3

And he said unto them, Go ye into all the world, and preach the gospel to every creature.

He that believeth and is baptized shall be saved; but he that believeth not shall be damned.

And these signs shall follow them that believe; In my name shall they cast out devils; they shall speak with new tongues;

They shall take up serpents; and if they drink any deadly thing, it shall not hurt them; they shall lay hands on the sick, and they shall recover.

So then after the Lord had spoken unto them, he was received up into heaven, and sat on the right hand of God.

And they went forth, and preached every where, the Lord working with them, and confirming the word with signs following. Amen.

Mark 16:15-20

But ye shall receive power, after that the Holy Ghost is come upon you: and ye shall be witnesses unto me both in Jerusalem, and in all Judaea, and in Samaria, and unto the uttermost part of the earth.

Acts 1:8

The Spirit of the Lord is upon me, because he hath anointed me to preach the gospel to the poor; he hath sent me to heal the brokenhearted, to preach deliverance to the captives, and recovering of sight to the blind, to set at liberty them that are bruised,

Luke 4:18

Verily, verily, I say unto you, He that believeth on me, the works that I do shall he do also; and greater works than these shall he do; because I go unto my Father.

John 14:12

And I say also unto thee, That thou art Peter, and upon this rock I will build my church; and the gates of hell shall not prevail against it.

And I will give unto thee the keys of the kingdom of heaven: and whatsoever thou shalt bind on earth shall be bound in heaven: and whatsoever thou shalt loose on earth shall be loosed in heaven.

Matthew 16:18, 19

A new commandment I give unto you, That ye love one another; as I have loved you, that ye also love one another.

By this shall all men know that ye are my disciples; if ye have love one to another.

John 13:34, 35

Beloved, let us love one another: for love is of God; and every one that loveth is born of God, and knoweth God.

And we have known and believed the love that God hath to us. God is love; and he that dwelleth in love dwelleth in God, and God in him.

Herein is our love made perfect, that we may have the boldness in the day of judgment: because as he is, so are we in this world.

I John 4:6, 16, 17

For whatsoever is born of God overcometh the world: and this is the victory that overcometh the world, even our faith.

Who is he that overcometh the world, but he that believeth that Jesus is the Son of God?

I John 5:4, 5

Now faith is the substance of things hoped for, the evidence of things not seen.

For by it the elders obtained a good report.

Through faith we understand that the worlds were framed by the word of God, so that things which are seen were not made of things which do appear.

Who through faith subdued kingdoms, wrought righteousness, obtained promises, stopped the mouths of lions,

Quenched the violence of fire, escaped the edge of the sword, out of weakness were made strong, waxed valiant in fight, turned to flight the armies of the aliens.

Hebrews 11:1-3, 33, 34

Ye are the salt of the earth:

Matthew 5:13a

For God so loved the world, that he gave his only begotten Son, that whosoever believeth in him should not perish, but have everlasting life.

John 3:16

Go ye therefore, and teach all nations, baptizing them in the name of the Father, and of the Son, and of the Holy Ghost:

Teaching them to observe all things whatsoever I have commanded you: and, lo, I am with you alway, even unto the end of the world. Amen.

Matthew 28:19, 20

Help Your Business

This book of the law shall not depart out of thy mouth; but thou shalt meditate therein day and night, that thou mayest observe to do according to all that is written therein: for then thou shalt make thy way prosperous, and then thou shalt have good success.

Joshua 1:8

Thus saith the Lord, thy Redeemer, the Holy One of Israel; I am the Lord thy God which teacheth thee to profit, which leadeth thee by the way that thou shouldest go.

Isaiah 48:17

Beloved, I wish above all things that thou mayest prosper and be in health, even as thy soul prospereth.

III John 2

But thou shalt remember the Lord thy God: for it is he that giveth thee power to get wealth, that he may establish his covenant which he sware unto thy fathers, as it is this day.

Deuteronomy 8:18

Trust in the Lord with all thine heart; and lean not unto thine own understanding.

In all thy ways acknowledge him, and he shall direct thy paths.

Be not wise in thine own eyes: fear the Lord, and depart from evil.

It shall be health to thy navel, and marrow to thy bones.

Honour the Lord with thy substance, and with the firstfruits of all thine increase:

So shall thy barns be filled with plenty, and thy presses shall burst out with new wine.

Proverbs 3:5-10

Then shalt thou prosper, if thou takest heed to fulfil the statutes and judgments which the Lord charged Moses with concerning Israel: be strong, and of good courage; dread not, nor be dismayed.

I Chronicles 22:13

Blessed is the man that walketh not in the counsel of the ungodly, nor standeth in the way of sinners, nor sitteth in the seat of the scornful.

But his delight is in the law of the Lord; and in his law doth he meditate day and night.

And he shall be like a tree planted by the rivers of water, that bringeth forth his fruit in his season; his leaf also shall not wither; and whatsoever he doeth shall prosper.

Psalm 1:1-3

And it shall come to pass, if thou shalt hearken diligently unto the voice of the Lord thy God, to observe and to do all his commandments which I command thee this day, that the Lord thy God will set thee on high above all nations of the earth:

And all these blessings shall come on thee, and overtake thee, if thou shalt hearken unto the voice of the Lord thy God.

Blessed shalt thou be in the city, and blessed shalt thou be in the field.

Blessed shall be the fruit of thy body, and the fruit of thy ground, and the fruit of thy cattle, the increase of thy kine, and the flocks of thy sheep.

Blessed shall be thy basket and thy store.

Blessed shalt thou be when thou comest in, and blessed shalt thou be when thou goest out.

The Lord shall command the blessing upon thee in thy storehouses, and in all that thou settest thine hand unto; and he shall bless thee in the land which the Lord thy God giveth thee.

And the Lord shall make thee plenteous in goods, in the fruit of thy body, and in the fruit of thy cattle, and in the fruit of thy ground, in the land which the Lord sware unto thy fathers to give thee.

The Lord shall open unto thee his good treasure, the heaven to give the rain unto thy land in his season, and to bless all the work of thine hand: and thou shalt lend unto many nations, and thou shalt not borrow.

And the Lord shall make thee the head, and not the tail; and thou shalt be above only, and thou shalt not be beneath; if thou hearken unto the commandments of the Lord thy God, which I command thee this day, to observe and to do them:

Deuteronomy 28:1-6, 8, 11-13

But seek ye first the kingdom of God, and his righteousness; and all these things shall be added unto you.

Matthew 6:33

Commit thy works unto the Lord, and thy thoughts shall be established.

Proverbs 16:3

Through wisdom is an house builded; and by understanding it is established:

And by knowledge shall the chambers be filled with all precious and pleasant riches.

Proverbs 24:3, 4

I go the way of all the earth: be thou strong therefore, and shew thyself a man;

And keep the charge of the Lord thy God, to walk in his ways, to keep his statutes, and his commandments, and his judgments, and his testimonies, as it is written in the law of Moses, that thou mayest prosper in all that thou doest, and whithersoever thou turnest thyself:

I Kings 2:2, 3

If they obey and serve him, they shall spend their days in prosperity, and their years in pleasures.

Job 36:11

Not slothful in business; fervent in spirit; serving the Lord;

Romans 12:11

Masters, give unto your servants that which is just and equal; knowing that ye also have a Master in heaven.

Colossians 4:1

...but we beseech you, brethren, that ye increase more and more;

And that ye study to be quiet, and to do your own business, and to work with your own hands, as we commanded you;

That ye may walk honestly toward them that are without, and that ye may have lack of nothing.

I Thessalonians 4:10b-12

WHAT YOU CAN DO TO
Please God

Even every one that is called by my name: for I have created him for my glory, I have formed him; yea, I have made him.

This people have I formed for myself, they shall shew forth my praise.

Isaiah 43:7, 21

But the hour cometh, and now is, when the true worshippers shall worship the Father in spirit and in truth: for the Father seeketh such to worship him.

God is a Spirit: and they that worship him must worship him in spirit and in truth.

John 4:23, 24

It came even to pass, as the trumpeters and singers were as one, to make one sound to be heard in praising and thanking the Lord; and when they lifted up their voice with the trumpets and cymbals and instruments of music, and praised the Lord, saying, For he is good; for his mercy endureth for ever: that then the house was filled with a cloud, even the house of the Lord,

So that the priests could not stand to minister by reason of the cloud: for the glory of the Lord had filled the house of God.

II Chronicles 5:13, 14

Ye also, as lively stones, are built up a spiritual house, an holy priesthood, to offer up spiritual sacrifices, acceptable to God by Jesus Christ.

But ye are a chosen generation, a royal priesthood, an holy nation, a peculiar people; that ye should shew forth the praises of him who hath called you out of darkness into his marvellous light:

I Peter 2:5, 9

By him therefore let us offer the sacrifice of praise to God continually, that is, the fruit of our lips giving thanks to his name.

But to do good and to communicate forget not: for with such sacrifices God is well pleased.

Hebrews 13:15, 16

Thou art worthy, O Lord, to receive glory and honour and power: for thou hast created all things, and for thy pleasure they are and were created.

Revelation 4:11

But without faith it is impossible to please him; for he that cometh to God must believe that he is, and that he is a rewarder of them that diligently seek him.

Hebrews 11:6

That ye might walk worthy of the Lord unto all pleasing, being fruiful in every good work, and increasing in the knowledge of God;

Colossians 1:10

I beseech you therefore, brethren, by the mercies of God, that ye present your bodies a living sacrifice, holy, acceptable unto God, which is your reasonable service.

And be not conformed to this world: but be ye transformed by the renewing of your mind, that ye may prove what is that good, and acceptable, and perfect, will of God.

Romans 12:1, 2

I exhort therefore, that, first of all, supplications, prayers, intercessions, and giving of thanks, be made for all men;

For this is good and acceptable in the sight of God our Saviour;

I will therefore that men pray every where, lifting up holy hands, without wrath and doubting.

I Timothy 2:1, 3, 8

My mouth shall speak the praise of the Lord: and let all flesh bless his holy name for ever and ever.

Psalm 145:21

I will greatly praise the Lord with my mouth; yea, I will praise him among the multitude.

Psalm 109:30

O Clap your hands, all ye people; shout unto God with the voice of triumph.

Psalm 47:1

The Lord taketh pleasure in them that fear him, in those that hope in his mercy.

Psalm 147:11

Praise ye the Lord. Sing unto the Lord a new song, and his praise in the congregation of saints.

Let Israel rejoice in him that made him: let the children of Zion be joyful in their King.

Let them praise his name in the dance: let them sing praises unto him with the timbrel and harp.

For the Lord taketh pleasure in his people: he will beautify the meek with salvation.

Let the saints be joyful in glory: let them sing aloud upon their beds.

Let the high praises of God be in their mouth,

Psalm 149:1-6a

So then they that are in the flesh cannot please God.

But ye are not in the flesh, but in the Spirit,

Romans 8:8, 9a

And whatsoever we ask, we receive of him, because we keep his commandments, and do those things that are pleasing in his sight.

I John 3:22

God's Plan Of Salvation . . .

GOD'S PLAN OF
Salvation

Wherefore, as by one man sin entered into the world, and death by sin; and so death passed upon all men, for that all have sinned:

Romans 5:12

For all have sinned, and come short of the glory of God;

Romans 3:23

For the wages of sin is death; but the gift of God is eternal life through Jesus Christ our Lord.

Romans 6:23

But God commendeth his love toward us, in that, while we were yet sinners, Christ died for us.

Romans 5:8

Moreover, brethren, I declare unto you the gospel which I preached unto you, which also ye have received, and wherein ye stand;

By which also ye are saved if ye keep in memory what I preached unto you, unless ye have believed in vain.

For I delivered unto you first of all that which I also received, how that Christ died for our sins according to the scriptures;

And that he was buried, and that he rose again the third day according to the scriptures;

I Corinthians 15:1-4

For God sent not his Son into the world to condemn the world; but that the world through him might be saved.

John 3:17

He that believeth on the Son hath everlasting life: and he that believeth not the Son shall not see life; but the wrath of God abideth on him.

John 3:36

For God so loved the world, that he gave his only begotten Son, that whosoever believeth in him should not perish, but have everlasting life.

John 3:16

But as many as received him, to them gave he power to become the sons of God, even to them that believe on his name:

John 1:12

For by grace are ye saved through faith; and that not of yourselves: it is the gift of God:
Not of works, lest any man should boast.

Ephesians 2:8, 9

Behold, I stand at the door, and knock: if any man hear my voice, and open the door, I will come in to him, and will sup with him, and he with me.

Revelation 3:20

But what saith it? The word is nigh thee, even in thy mouth, and in thy heart: that is, the word of faith, which we preach;

That if thou shalt confess with thy mouth the Lord Jesus, and shalt believe in thine heart that God hath raised him from the dead, thou shalt be saved.

For with the heart man believeth unto righteousness; and with the mouth confession is made unto salvation.

Romans 10:8-10

Whosoever therefore shall confess me before men, him will I confess also before my Father which is in heaven.

Matthew 10:32

And this is the record, that God hath given to us eternal life, and this life is in his Son.

He that hath the Son hath life; and he that hath not the Son of God hath not life.

These things have I written unto you that believe on the name of the Son of God; that ye may know that ye have eternal life, and that ye may believe on the name of the Son of God.

I John 5:11-13

MY PRAYER LIST

MY PRAYER LIST

_____
_____
_____
_____
_____
_____
_____
_____
_____
_____
_____
_____
_____
_____
_____
_____
_____
_____
_____
_____
_____
_____
_____
_____
_____
_____
_____
_____
_____
_____

MY PRAYER LIST

_____
_____
_____
_____
_____
_____
_____
_____
_____
_____
_____
_____
_____
_____
_____
_____
_____
_____
_____
_____
_____
_____
_____
_____
_____
_____
_____
_____
_____
_____
_____
_____
_____
_____

MY PRAYER LIST

_____
_____
_____
_____
_____
_____
_____
_____
_____
_____
_____
_____
_____
_____
_____
_____
_____
_____
_____
_____
_____
_____
_____
_____
_____
_____
_____
_____
_____
_____
_____

MY PRAYER LIST

_____
_____
_____
_____
_____
_____
_____
_____
_____
_____
_____
_____
_____
_____
_____
_____
_____
_____
_____
_____
_____
_____
_____
_____
_____
_____
_____
_____
_____
_____

MY PRAYER LIST

_____
_____
_____
_____
_____
_____
_____
_____
_____
_____
_____
_____
_____
_____
_____
_____
_____
_____
_____
_____
_____
_____
_____
_____
_____
_____
_____
_____
_____
_____
_____
_____

MY PRAYER LIST

_____

_____

_____

_____

_____

_____

_____

_____

_____

_____

_____

_____

_____

_____

_____

_____

_____

_____

_____

_____

_____

_____

_____

_____

_____

_____

_____

_____

_____

MY PRAYER LIST

_____
_____
_____
_____
_____
_____
_____
_____
_____
_____
_____
_____
_____
_____
_____
_____
_____
_____
_____
_____
_____
_____
_____
_____
_____
_____
_____
_____
_____
_____
_____

MY PRAYER LIST

PERSONAL STUDY NOTES

PERSONAL STUDY NOTES

PERSONAL STUDY NOTES

PERSONAL STUDY NOTES

PERSONAL STUDY NOTES

PERSONAL STUDY NOTES

PERSONAL STUDY NOTES

PERSONAL STUDY NOTES

PERSONAL STUDY NOTES